AF837301

Online Community Therapy

Online Community Therapy

The Support Network

Will Henderson and Mary Jackson Pitts

LEXINGTON BOOKS
Lanham • Boulder • New York • London

Published by Lexington Books
An imprint of The Rowman & Littlefield Publishing Group, Inc.
4501 Forbes Boulevard, Suite 200, Lanham, Maryland 20706
www.rowman.com

86-90 Paul Street, London EC2A 4NE

Copyright © 2022 by The Rowman & Littlefield Publishing Group, Inc.

All rights reserved. No part of this book may be reproduced in any form or by any electronic or mechanical means, including information storage and retrieval systems, without written permission from the publisher, except by a reviewer who may quote passages in a review.

British Library Cataloguing in Publication Information Available

Library of Congress Cataloging-in-Publication Data

Names: Henderson, Will (Online communities advocate) author. | Jackson Pitts, Mary, author.
Title: Online community therapy : the support network / Will Henderson and Mary Jackson Pitts.
Description: Lanham : Lexington Books, [2022] | Includes bibliographical references and index. | Summary: "This book explores how online therapy communities offer an accessible space that is not confined by economic abilities, geographical barriers, or familial restraints. Scholars of communication, sociology, and psychology will find this book of particular interest"— Provided by publisher.
Identifiers: LCCN 2022031386 (print) | LCCN 2022031387 (ebook) | ISBN 9781793631022 (cloth) | ISBN 9781793631039 (ebook)
Subjects: LCSH: Internet in psychotherapy. | Online social networks
Classification: LCC RC489.I54 H46 2022 (print) | LCC RC489.I54 (ebook) | DDC 302.23/1—dc23/eng/20220812
LC record available at https://lccn.loc.gov/2022031386
LC ebook record available at https://lccn.loc.gov/2022031387

Contents

Acknowledgments

WILL HENDERSON

This book would not have been possible without the continual support of my wife, Mary Kathryn. Thanks for your encouragement and for listening to me talk things out regarding this research and my ideas. To our two sons, Oden and Otto, thanks for providing humor and joy in my life. After reading countless stories and posts regarding the subject manner, I could always count on you two to bring me joy.

I would also like to thank my colleagues at Clemson University who shared valuable input in the research design and analysis. I greatly appreciate your assistance. Thanks to Diane Walters for your editing work and Rob Yeo for the cover artwork. Thank you to all the professors at Arkansas State University who watched this research develop. A special thank you to my coauthor, Dr. Mary Jackson-Pitts, who has presented this research and played a significant role in my thesis development, as well as with this book. This wouldn't have been a reality without your guidance.

I would also like to dedicate this research to my friends who have suffered from suicidal ideation, depression, and self-harm. Though many of you are no longer with us, your memory lives on. More specifically, friends from high school who have taken their own lives and suffered from behaviors mentioned in this book—Anna, Jason, Matt, and Stacie. Miss you all.

MARY JACKSON PITTS, PHD

Our lives are enriched by those who have lifted us up in a multitude of our journeys. Media, while often criticized for its shortcomings, can be used to share knowledge, enrich lives, and be used as a tool to create communities of support and learning. Nonlinear multimedia platforms can be used successfully to build others up in the journey with self-damaging thoughts and behaviors. To be able to help others has always been my expectation of media's power. The contents of this book support the positive role media can play in our lives. The discoveries in this research are in part possible because of the strong support system that I have had in my career.

To my family, Stephen, Lillie, and Sarah, thank you for providing me the time and opportunity to devote to this research, and to my colleagues at Arkansas State University, thank you for doing the work required, so that I could focus on the contents of this book. And, I thank the many students that I have taught over time, who serve as the inspiration to continue to love learning new things. More specifically, thank you to my coauthor and former student Will Henderson who provided the foundation for this research and carries the same passion for finding ways to help people.

Chapter 1

Finding Help Online

Imagine finding a place where people find the support needed to divert self-harming thoughts or behaviors. This place/space would not be limited by economic abilities, geographical barriers, or familial restraints. Online therapy communities can be used as a modality to assist people in dealing with struggles of self-harming thoughts and behaviors. As media researchers, the authors set out to better understand how social media can play a positive role for individuals needing help when common barriers might stop them from finding support as they struggle with self-harm. Social media has provided an opportunity for users to create online therapy communities where members create communities to share experiences, provide support, and provide a listening ear to those who are in crisis. Individuals seek these communities to find personal connections, develop communal bonding, and help in providing behavioral interruptions and modifications that help members avoid self-harm.

Studying online therapy communities by examining member motivations for joining such groups is the focus of this research. Using mixed methodologies of self-administered surveys and in-depth interviews have provided the authors with the opportunity to explore how therapy communities can be used as a tool in the overall care of individuals who are in crisis and dealing with self-harming thoughts and behaviors. Faced with issues of no care because of monetary constraints, lack of insurance coverage, or close connections, who have no experience in addressing self-harming behaviors, members share perspectives and insights into how online therapy communities may be helpful. Through users gathering in the community, individuals are motivated to join, engage, and support other members while seeking help for themselves. The online therapy communities provide a sense of belonging, a knowledge that thoughts and behaviors are common among other members and that there are ways to address such thoughts and behaviors with the help of community members.

Self-damaging behaviors, such as suicide and other mental disorders, have been rising in the past years. In 2018, the United States alone had 16.2 million adults, 6.7 percent of the country's adult population, experiencing a moment of depression (Morin 2019). While depressive conditions continue to increase in adults, younger demographics are experiencing a more significant increase in psychological distress. In using the Kessler Psychological Distress Scale (K6), researchers found a 78 percent increase in the psychological distress of twenty- to twenty-one-year-olds compared with those in 2008 (Twenge et al. 2019). While several factors could contribute to the rise, Twenge et al. (2019) believed that this could be due to increased digital media consumption and the impact it has had on changing commonly used social interaction. Ivey-Stephenson et al.'s 2020 report from the Center for Disease Control and Prevention (CDC) stated that 18.8 percent of students, ages fourteen to eighteen, who were surveyed as part of the Youth Risk Behavior Surveillance Study, had considered suicide. And, when gender was the primary variable associated with suicide consideration, 24.1 percent of females had considered suicide. Data from this study showed increases in attempted suicides by 2.6 percent from 2008 to 2019 with a 2.9 percent increase among females. Females thought more about suicide, planned suicide, and had attempted suicide more often than males. What was found among males was that as they became older, they were more likely to consider or make suicide plans. The CDC suggested that suicide prevention programs should be tailored to specific ages and gender. Because suicide is a leading cause of death among teens, Ivey-Stephenson et al. (2020) suggested that the prevention of self-damaging behaviors that can lead to suicide should be a top public health priority, and a comprehensive approach is needed to help young and old deal with suicidal thoughts. This approach should use a variety of health-care modalities that traditionally have been used and other support measures. Beyond the traditional forms of support for people dealing with self-harming thoughts and behaviors is a nontraditional approach, which is the subject of this book. The authors believe that tools yet to be used that can be found among peers and mentors should be considered as resources to change the trajectory of loss of life or physical impairment. This book explores the relationships between online therapy groups and self-damaging thoughts and behaviors.

With the continual increase in self-damaging behaviors, there is an opportunity for social media users to find a place of belonging in a healthy online community. In this research, self-damaging behaviors are defined as any behavior that can impact oneself from harm to their being. This definition includes, but is not limited to, eating disorders, depression, suicidal thoughts, anxiety, post-traumatic stress disorder (PTSD), or drug addiction.

With the increase in self-damaging behaviors, online platforms continue to rise in the number of users. In the 2012 "Quarter 3 Investor Report," Facebook stated that they reached one billion users, while at the end of 2020, Facebook had reached 2.79 billion monthly users (Iqbal 2021). Facebook continues to be the choice platform among adults, with 69 percent of US adult users in 2021 (Auxier and Anderson 2021), while 2 percent of 9,800 US teens identified Facebook as their platform of choice (Sandler 2020). Online communities expand farther than just Facebook and Instagram. Platforms also could be self-identifying or anonymous. Both types of platforms have existing limitations and facilitators that users considered when choosing a platform. The anonymous online community platform Reddit measured fifty-two million active users in 2020 (Hutchinson 2020). With the increase of users, social media platforms have facilitated online communities as tools for connecting and interacting with peers and like-minded users (Valkenburg and Piotrowski 2017).

As culture progresses, mental health worsens: "Rates of youth with severe depression increased from 5.9 percent in 2012 to 8.2 percent in 2015. Even with severe depression, 76 percent of youth are left with no or insufficient treatment" (Reinert, Nguyen, and Fritze 2017, para. 3). With the increase in damaging behaviors and online communities, there is potential to combine the two ideas to create a complementary therapy method. This is not to substitute traditional treatment from professional counseling but to facilitate an online environment where the users' gratifications are fulfilled.

Users collaborate with social media either by quantitative (likes and shares) or qualitative methods (comments). In prior research, it was found that the quantity of users' actions, such as liking and posting on social media, does not lead to low self-esteem or an unhealthy view of oneself (Shakya and Christakis 2017). However, Shakya and Christakis (2017) recognized that the quality of online interactions determined the impact on the user. Results concluded that online activity does not serve as a substitute for physical interactions, and such interactions are not as important as users may think. However, the researchers believed that healthy qualitative engagements could occur through an online community for individuals in limiting behavior situations. In this case, behaviors may limit one from pursuing physical relationships where online interactions could transition.

For life-altering changes to happen, users must engage in a community platform that fits their needs and gratifications. Users must become loyal to the platform in regard to their engagement. They can then collaborate on posts that discuss self-damaging behaviors. Loyalty creates repeat visitors to the platform for further engagement. Previous research found that loyalty in the users occurred if a sense of belonging was present (Liu and Guo 2015). In Liu and Guo's 2015 research, trust in the site was found to support the sense of belonging but did not impact loyalty to the platform. Out of the constructs in Liu and Guo's research, service quality and a sense of belonging supported loyalty to a platform (2015).

In addition to the sense of belonging, Facebook provides utilities to create groups around diverse topics. Lijadi and van Schalkwyk created Facebook groups for children who live a high-travel lifestyle. The researchers found that as the children engaged with one another, "interaction could be intense" (2015, 7). While users shared life experiences in the Facebook group, it provided a sense of trust in the community, despite the geographical constraints that existed in this group. Gaining trust in social media communities was essential as users encountered their self-damaging behaviors. Building trust in online communities would fulfill the gratification of desiring to be accepted. Trust would also mitigate the common fear of cyberbullying commonly found in users among teenagers diagnosed with anxiety (Calancie et al. 2017). While the world is interconnected through online communities, mental health professionals still face the reality of increased behaviors (Morin 2019).

The connection between mental well-being and social media usage is apparent due to the evolving methods of communication over the last couple of decades. Social media communities have provided different friendship forms through digital bonds and sometimes progressed toward a physical relationship. In providing a digital community on social media, having relationships has led to both positive and negative impacts on the receiver of the communication message. Social media groups provide a sense of personal belonging with friends that users have never met in real life but have only met in the cyber world. This has created a physically connected society to be more digitally connected, creating a worldwide network.

According to Lijadi and van Schalkwyk, community groups allow users to share information that would benefit the group. Interaction also would "raise awareness on certain issues related to special interest group description or purpose" (2015, 2). Users could also ask questions, listen to other perspectives that would assist in their understanding, and meet other people who engage in the same behaviors. While a sense of ownership and trust is essential to engage with the community, hope for recovery through mutual help and support is another critical factor (Liu and Guo 2015; Lijadi and van Schalkwyk 2015; Robinson 1988). Previous research also found that online communities provided additional psychological factors, such as "a sense of control, self-confidence, feelings of more independence, social interactions, and improved feelings" (Barak, Boniel-Nissim, and Suler 2008).

The research here will be accomplished through a post-positivism view and will apply the uses and gratifications theory through a grounded theory approach. In efforts to apply the uses and gratifications framework in conjunction with this research, this theory needs to be defined. According to Papacharissi (2009), the uses and gratifications theory focuses on the main motivations as to why users select and digest the content that they each, individually, seek out to fulfill their unique gratifications desired. Each desired gratification is specific to the individual, themselves, and their diverse set of social and psychological characteristics. In this case, users may seek out communities that fulfill the motivations of trust and secrecy.

Chapter 2

Why Communities Matter

The purpose of this research is to better understand how individuals who have self-damaging behaviors may use online communities to help with their mental health journey. In the communities, users can seek like-minded individuals who may share similar struggles of behavior-focused characteristics that could be damaging to oneself (Kingod et al. 2017). The researchers apply the uses and gratifications theory as a theoretical understanding of this study. This research does not propose online communities as a replacement for licensed therapy for the behaviors but rather investigates a support system that was previously not available in the pre-social media era. Through the uses and gratifications theory, the researchers suspect online groups can be used as a supplement to professional therapy or even as a first step to recovery (Kingod et al. 2017).

By becoming involved with other people online, users may be able to act in a way that constantly deepens and develops their own personal growth, based on the affirmation of other users (Isaranon 2019). Isaranon's 2019 findings supported that Facebook users who found affirmation online reported a higher level of self-esteem. The affirmation found in online communities is originally brought from the union of romantic relationships and the self-fulfillment that romance offers (Isaranon 2019; Kumashiro et al. 2007). Healthy Facebook communities allow the users to enhance personal growth, trust, affirmation, and other traits of bonded relationships. While Facebook communities operate differently than other online communities, the main principles of a healthy online community remain the same. Principles of healthy communities, regardless of the model, are founded on trust and communal bonds.

Critiques of social media include findings of increased Facebook usage when thoughts of loneliness or worry are heightened in the user. In previous research, it was found that heightened activity on social media could result in a decline in the user's mental state and well-being (Kross et al. 2013). However, the researchers believe that social media could offer benefits that could provide an optimistic view regarding social media usage. Therefore, as social media use is studied, online therapy groups must be explored to help create communities focused on well-being. This brings culture to a deciding point where embracing therapeutic online groups becomes inevitable to create a sense of belonging and ownership for users who suffer from self-damaging struggles.

According to the National Institute of Mental Health (2021), 51.5 million adults in the United States were impacted by mental illness in 2019. This research would encourage these individuals to engage with healthy online social media communities that are focused on specific self-damaging behaviors.

The problem of increased cases of depression and mental illness in America is alarming. As a result, the number of individuals who need professional help will continue to increase. When it comes to professional help and the individuals who need this help, as they struggle with self-damaging behaviors, there are barriers that may prevent them from receiving adequate assistance. On top of the stigma surrounding mental health issues and the lack of education among the public, another barrier is the ability to pay for mental health care through insurance. In 2004, 87 percent of one thousand randomly selected Americans stated that lack of insurance prevented people from receiving mental health treatment; in addition to the lack of insurance, cost concerns were prevalent with 81 percent of the polled audience (Chamberlin 2004). While cases of behaviors continue to increase yearly, the number of behavior-focused social media communities is growing.

There are numerous Facebook groups that serve as a place of community for users dealing with eating disorders, depression, anxiety, and other mental health concerns. Though the groups have large communities, engagement with members may be difficult for many users. In 2020, social media audiences increased to over three-point-eight-billion, which was a result of a 9 percent increase compared to 2019 (Kemp 2020). In 2018, 51 percent of a polled audience between ages eighteen to twenty-four stated that social media would be hard to give up (Smith and Anderson 2018). This frequent use of social media allows users countless opportunities for engagements that fulfill the gratifications sought from a health community. Daily social media activity could provide the benefits of immediate gratification from an online community.

As with most media platforms, researchers seem to begin first by looking at the adverse impact media content can have on users (Schramm, Parker, and Lylē 1961; Bandura 1965; Cater and Strickland 1975; Holden, 1972; Gerbner et al. 1986; Carey 1989). Yet, media content can deliver positive experiences for users when they engage (Mares and Pan 2013; Anderson and Jiang 2018; Clark, Algoe, and Green 2018). While legacy media and its impact on mental health have been widely studied, the problem that exists is the lack of research using social media as a complementary type of therapy for individuals struggling with self-damaging behaviors. Through the increase in this knowledge and the findings from both qualitative and quantitative studies in the present research, online social media communities may soon be recognized for their potential to provide the important gratifications sought from individuals suffering from self-damaging behaviors. This could have life-impacting results for the users, as they would be able to find a cost-friendly, connected, and trusted community on a platform they use daily.

CONTEXT OF STUDY

Justification

The findings from this work may alter how we, as a society, can use non-legacy media, such as social media channels, for the betterment of human behavior. According to the Anxiety and Depression Association of America (ADAA), 18 percent of the US population who are eighteen and older—an estimated forty million people—struggle with depression or other types of anxiety disorders (ADAA 2021). This creates a need for therapy through professional or digital means. Even while self-damaging behavior communities are active, the increase of these behaviors continues to rise, with an alarming one hundred thirty suicides per day in America, as reported by the American Foundation for Suicide Prevention (AFSP 2019). The AFSP continued to report that suicide is the tenth leading cause of death, and in 2019 alone, forty-seven five hundred eleven Americans committed suicide. As a result of increased behaviors, such as depression and suicidal thoughts, there is a large percentage of people who have searched online for medical advice and have been exposed to mass media communication regarding this topic. "Many youth use the Internet as a means to obtain information and resources about depression and other issues that may be difficult to discuss with people in their off-line lives" (Lerman et al. 2017, 721). The impact could provide efforts to decrease damaging behaviors in the individuals. Nesi wrote,

> The public and highly accessible nature of social media also creates the possibility for establishing new connections online. This may provide opportunities to receive online social support for certain youth, particularly those who may not readily have access to communities of similar peers. (2020, 119)

Though the research conclusion would not create a substitute for a physical community or professional therapy, it could serve as an introduction to recovery.

The researchers believe that the uses and gratifications theory would best support this type of research. Blumler (1979) suggested that media users intentionally seek content to satisfy their needs. Often, the content is selectively chosen, and each individual user may construct their own meaning from the information sought. Through storytelling, the community provides an opportunity for experienced users to become opinion leaders who can provide emotional support to impacted members (Greene et al. 2011). Through finding an online community and using a social media platform, users are exposed to voices that may have previously sought out professional help, allowing the experienced voices to share advice and secondhand recovery treatment with the users. This idea applies to Katz, Gurevitch, and Haas's (1973) suggestion to use an interactive process with media content where cognition occurs when information is gathered, processed through behaviors, and then used to deal with emotions, pleasures, and feelings (1973). The online community provides the benefit of social interaction with those who have had prior experiences with self-damaging behaviors (Rovai 2002).

A sense of belonging has been studied in online communities, such as various Facebook groups, that provided support for individuals who are grieving as loved ones underwent hospice treatment (Oliver et al. 2015). In a blog post sharing the lived experience, blogger Riley Lee shared their experience with an online support community:

> Six months after I lost my mother, my nasty friends, anxiety, and PTSD were back in full force. I was done. I was at an all-time low. Nothing could help me. My husband was supportive, and I saw my therapist every week. Yet, nothing made me feel better. I was/am in a deep, dark hole. I wanted to die by suicide. Then, I found, by chance, a closed group on Facebook. These women are my kind of women. They were honest, have no regrets for being themselves, and speak their truth. I felt like I belonged there. I can be me with no regrets and no worries of being judged. (Lee 2017, para. 1–3)

Face-to-face support groups around health issues have commonly been used in the effort to create a form of therapy (Kessler, Mickelson, and Zhao 1997, as cited in Wright et al. 2003). Nesi (2020) suggested that the constraints of finding people in a local geographic community who are working through similar mental health issues can make it difficult for individuals to find the support needed. Thus, online communities may offer help beyond geographic constraints. Previous research showed that online communities allowed users to engage without geographical constraints, which created a worldwide community around the common bond of certain behaviors (Mickelson 1997; Weinberg et al. 1995, as cited in Wright et al. 2003).

Online support groups have the potential to help users with self-confidence, depression, and other struggles defined by the needs of the group. While considering behaviors such as PTSD, self-harming behaviors, and suicidal thoughts, this study seeks to discover the gratification of involvement in the communities. Based on this research, users' involvement in an online community could develop a larger community base founded on similar qualities of the original user. In a study recently done to measure the social media impact on people who were living with AIDS/HIV, it was found that diagnosed individuals who were involved in a community-based social media society would more likely share relatable information than those not involved in the community (Chen and Shi 2015). Social media communities share their own lived experience connecting the common bond between all members.

The experience of Marissa Brennan describes the communal bond found in the community. When she was diagnosed with endometriosis, Brennan found an online support group that was targeted toward women who were diagnosed with this disease. Through the engagement in the community, she found shared common interests provided support and resources (Willis 2018). Through these examples, one can see the impact of social media-based communities on people dealing with a variety of struggles. Through the completion of this research, the findings may impact the future of therapy and health care and provide other avenues to provide a higher quality of life. Examining online therapy communities led the researchers to a two-pronged research approach to better understand how online communities could make a positive difference in the lives of the people who joined the groups. Using quantitative and qualitative approaches, the researchers focused the research on six research questions and four hypotheses.

Research Questions

Q1: Do the participants feel that they are in a community that protects users' well-being?

Q2: What motivations are sought out in using online communities, either anonymous or identifying platforms?

Q3: Have self-damaging behaviors increased or decreased after interacting with behavior-focused online communities?

Q4: Are participants involved in both professional therapy and online communities?

Q5: What are social media users saying about online communities dedicated to self-damaging behaviors?

Q6: What guidelines are in place in communities to prevent toxicity in online communities?

Hypothesis

H1: Being engaged with an online support group will decrease thoughts about harmful behaviors.

As social support increases overall well-being (Buglass et al. 2017; Smith et al. 2021), harmful thoughts may decrease as relationships are developed. The well-being could occur at a higher rate when exercised in a group therapy environment (Ambrose 2011), such as a group focused on self-harm recovery.

H2: Being engaged with an online support group will create feelings of support within the online community.

As Facebook increases feelings of connection in various parts of life, individuals have found that social media allows them to develop both physical and digital relationships (Ferris and Hollenbaugh 2018). Through these relationships, high self-esteem will result as they find a sense of belonging, trust in the community, and hope for recovery.

H3: Groups over common bonds, such as a common diagnosis, will create a more connected and supportive group due to common life-impacting situations.

In previous research on Facebook groups that were focused on youth depression, it was found that the community provided "a positive, safe, and nonjudgmental environment to allow for self-disclosure and connections between like-minded youth" (Lerman et al. 2017, 734). Through a common bond of a diagnosis, individuals will find a community that provides the engagement needed for social support and empathy.

H4: Engagement in an online support group will increase emotional openness in social media users.

Individuals who are seeking assistance regarding sadness, stress, and/or anger are encountering various types of available communities (Lerman et al. 2017). In a search for assistance, current search results are in the form of digital content, online support groups, and blogs. While many of the results may provide a beneficial response, online communities are the only opportunity for users to receive social support from others regarding their behaviors (Lerman et al. 2017).

Chapter 3

Community Evolution

Communities develop over time as people find others who share similar experiences. The sharing of experiences has long been embedded in culture. In some form or another, communities have formed a common bond between individuals. This common bond, or "common spirit," in Hillery's (1955) terms, has created friendships and groups to live life in the world together. Communities have contributed to the social and cultural capital of a society. Online communities have the same capital that is commonly referenced by sociologists: built capital refers to the infrastructure of the online community. Social capital references the bonding of the users in the network. Cultural capital is the accumulation of all backgrounds of the users.

According to Bourdieu (1986), cultural capital exists as the embodied, the objectified, and the institutionalized state. The cultural capital is created through the user's background and lived experience. Through online communities, that cultural capital is displayed through the sharing of information and storytelling. To understand the beginnings, one must start at an early version of community.

Religion has always served as a place of community as it developed a high level of influence in the world. In religious literature, the common bond has shown to be an effective form of community. Individuals living in geographical locations, such as Egypt, Israel, and Samaria, created communities based around their geographic area and built capital of the area. This location-based bond resulted in subgroups that are mentioned in texts, like the Bible and the Torah. Throughout religious literature, several of these communities had quarrels with each other, such as the battle between the Israelite and the Philistine communities. Battles throughout the Old Testament were based on geographical dominion between community groups. Bourdieu (1986) described this as social domination—one group sought to force their values on all groups. However, the religious texts continue to provide examples of community therapy where individuals would gather under a common bond with trust in the community. In these communities, stories and resources were shared with each other (Mark 14:12–26; Matt. 17; Luke 10:38–42 New International Version (NIV)). This allowed every individual to be heard and understood while sharing their own needs together. The group around a communal bond of a religious figure proved to provide trust and hope in the advice sought.

Sixteen hundred years later, a group with similar religious beliefs became disappointed with the Church of England, as they believed that the idea of membership went against their own biblical convictions (The Gilder Lehrman Institute of American History 2013). This group bonded together two cultural capital values: religion and desire for freedom. As a group, they formed a community to create solutions for problematic topics that they all faced. This relationally intimate group provided a form of community where they offered support for each other that eventually initiated actions of searching for religious freedom (History.com Editors 2010). As the mentioned groups found a common bond with each other, gratifications were found that they were no longer facing issues alone. They were able to share life experiences in an open environment within the community.

TÖNNIES TYPES OF COMMUNITIES

German sociologist Ferdinand Tönnies suggested that social groups exist as two types of communities: "Gemeinschaft and Gesellschaft." These communities are diametrically different. Gemeinschaft is defined as the village life or community, while Gesellschaft is considered the urban environment or society (Tönnies 1957; Douglas 2010). With Gemeinschaft, members may often interact face-to-face within larger in person group settings, much like some communities where everyone knows your name. Members in Gemeinschaft are connected by common beliefs, frequent interaction, and familiarity with each other (Brint 2001).

In Tönnies's 1957 research, the Gesellschaft urban environment classified social interactions as distant and did not provide strong ties to its community members. Brint shared that Gesellschaft included uncommon beliefs, infrequent interaction, and competition (2001). Gesellschaft is the natural processing of culture and the world. The urban environment is not connected with bonds or trust. The urban members are actively changing lifestyles, habits, gratifications, and more. They are considered a society with everyone serving and requiring different needs and gratifications.

Tönnies explains in *Community and Society*,

> Gemeinschaft among people is stronger there and more alive; it is the lasting and genuine form of living together. In contrast to Gemeinschaft, Gesellschaft is transitory and superficial. Accordingly, Gemeinschaft should be understood as a living organism, Gesellschaft as a mechanical aggregate and artifact. (Tönnies 1957, 35)

Gemeinschaft villages are founded on simplicity. This type of community is studied as a small group of individuals who have some familiarity with each other and may have a common way of life and beliefs (Douglas 2010). The villages are the subgroups of the overall urban environment (Tönnies 1957). In simpler terms, students may enroll in a university (Gesellschaft). Through the existence of the student body, one may pursue to take part in smaller villages (Gemeinschaft) through intramural sports, clubs, or even classes. Each village has its own culture and set of normalities that are celebrated or honored.

In the digital world, Facebook, Reddit, and Twitter platforms are classified as Gesellschaft communities. The smaller villages of groups, subreddits—a forum dedicated to a specific topic on the website Reddit—and Twitter lists are Gemeinschaft communities (Lexico 2022). Social media platforms provide a range of interest groups that focus on any topic of interest to the members of the group. The Gemeinschaft members are seeking close ties with individuals with a common interest (Douglas 2010), while the greater online platform is the society. Tönnies's approach to communities is applicable within the frame of social media and its groups as a therapeutic approach (1957). The current online culture has a mixture of both types of communities that serve different purposes. Using Facebook's newsfeed is a key example of the urban environment society. It is an ever-changing resource of information, news, and highlights from other lived experiences.

This society presents challenges as users are not physically or emotionally connected with everyone on their friends' lists. The relationships are loosely connected, only by a friend's request. Users can contribute to other users' newsfeeds, but every update is a small percentage of what is seen in the posted timeframe. Users' posts compete with business pages, public groups, media outlets, and sponsored ads. As a result, all posts create a loose network of connections. Through online therapy groups, when someone joins a group, the members can build stronger connections because the members are there seeking gratifications from a communal-bond group. Facebook groups include posts made by members inside the group, which could include connected friends. This keeps the content of the group focused on the members joined. While members may be separated by geographic distance in online communities, they may find the engagement and interaction gratification that they have been seeking in the Facebook therapy group.

HILLERY'S DEFINITION OF COMMUNITIES

Apart from understanding the differences in society and villages, it is important to analyze the elements that define a community. Each Gemeinschaft has a connection point that bonds them as individuals. Sociologist George Hillery (1955) analyzed ninety-four contextual definitions for *community*. The articles included were analyzed through qualitative and quantitative measures.

Hillery found that there are two types of community: generic community and rural community. The generic community was a common theme with two sub-themes: (1) social interaction and (2) ecological relationships. Social interaction communities were bonded through the geographic area or presence of a common characteristic. The top contextual definitions in the social interaction communities were "possession of common ends, norms, means" (n = 20), and "common life" (n = 9) (1955, 114).

Online communities that were founded around self-damaging behaviors are bonded by common characteristics. Engagement in groups creates the dialogic nature of the behavioral-impacted life. Within a rural community, Hillery (1955) found that social interaction was the only theme defining the localized community. Social interaction within a rural community included self-sufficiency, common life, and locality. At the same time, the measure of locality had the highest number of definitions (n = 5). Within online communities, locality as a barrier is removed, which allows for greater engagement within the community where members find support when dealing with self-damaging behaviors.

The element of geographic area and locality group is evident in Facebook groups, such as *community parent* groups. As localized communities create a sense of community, social interactions will organically increase (Kim and Kaplan 2004). Through the community parent Facebook groups, individuals establish a connection through common characteristics such as sex, demographics, or profession. Through Hillery's (1955) definition of common life, another community example would include the subreddit r/Accounting. The description states the specific profession most users meet or are interested in: "Primarily for accountants and aspiring accountants to learn about and discuss their career choice" (Reddit 2009a). The communal bond of life as an accountant provides a sense of community for the user engaging in the subreddit. Hillery's definitions of community provide contextual definitions of how users may engage in online groups.

As history progressed, researchers started to explore how community groups could provide a form of therapy. The early group therapy practitioner Joseph Pratt implemented a form of group therapy for tuberculosis patients at Massachusetts General Hospital (Ambrose 2011). Patients were given instructions for bed rest and to live in outdoor sleeping areas. The diagnosed patients were then given a journal where they could track their hour-by-hour activities. When the patients would gather for a group meeting, they were instructed to share their lived experiences from their journals. Pratt named the early group therapy program the "class method" (Ambrose 2011). Through this class, he began to see an increased improvement in the well-being of the patients involved. Being in the group and the emotional support found, lent itself to assist community members with physical health and reduced emotional stressors.

With Pratt's community, participants were encouraged by more experienced members of the group to continue with the unique treatment (Ambrose 2011). While members were sleeping in outside sleeping venues, the experience provided an opportunity for the group to create a common bond and trust with each other. This unity in the group allowed an increase in healthy morale, which, as a result, created a healthier group. Since early group therapy work, medical professionals have been involved with similar methods where success was found. This has since transitioned leadership roles from the medical practitioners leading formal group therapy to social media users creating online communities.

COMMUNITY GRATIFICATIONS

Communities have been studied by scholars across many disciplines. Communities are found in clubs, social organizations, religious organizations, schools, businesses, and groups of friends. These community members come together for face-to-face meetings of engagement, resulting in the sharing of lived experiences. According to Douglas, communities could be defined as "'community spirit' or 'connected community'" (2010, 1). In addition to the community at large, smaller communities have provided a stronger sense of belonging around an association of social or cultural capital (Brint 2001).

Communities often provide a safe space for people to talk about their problems and receive support, but many individuals who would benefit from this support find themselves unable to participate in face-to-face meetings because of barriers such as transportation, scheduling, and/or finding safe places to meet. Online communities have no such barriers and also provide anonymity and confidentiality. As a result of anonymity, openness is encouraged in the community (Strand, Eng, and Gammon 2020). Due to the technological advances in social media platforms, online communities have facilitated participation opportunities in groups where users can find engagement gratification.

Discovering groups that can provide support for self-harming behaviors is often made difficult within small cities and towns because of the lack of support groups. The lack of groups that encourage openness is even more evident in larger cities, where individuals are less likely to know their neighbors and community members. Confidence in confidentiality remains important to the participants (Strand, Eng, and Gammon 2020). Online groups provide individuals with communities that are usually not available within a person's geographical location.

Tech-savvy millennials and the Generation Z population engage with social media communities that provide entertainment and surveillance gratifications. Likewise, these community members can engage with groups that can provide encouragement gratification for a myriad of mental health issues, including self-harming behaviors. While various age demographics may have differing responses, active social media users are pleased with the results. In a recent interview, eighteen-year-old Andrew Kowalski responded,

> The older generation, they don't really think that technology is great because it takes away the eye contact and communication from person to person. Now it's a lot of technology-to-person instead of face-to-face contact. They see that as hiding behind a phone. I think it's good, though, because you're able to access any information at any time you want. (Brownstein 2015, para. 7)

While most online groups do not have the duality of face-to-face meetings with online communities, users receive a different gratification . . . knowledge-seeking gratification (Strand, Eng, and Gammon 2020).

Online community members can share their stories and often find answers to questions related to their experiences. While this is the current reality of the social media landscape, there are several types of communities that provide diverse options for users. Social media participants are now able to find communities focused on a host of topics, located anywhere and for any cause.

According to the first level of Brint's developed typology, the basis of the relationship is dependent on geography or choice. In the context of self-damaging behaviors, the basis of choice of engagement correctly defines the communities studied (2001). Brint's second level in the typology shows that the primary reason for interaction is belief-based or activity-based (2001). As communal bond, trust, hope, and self-confidence are met in the communities, they serve as the foundational reasons for interaction. The typology splits the community by the location of other members. Also, in Brint's typology, online communities are classified as "Imagined Communities" (2001). This type of community is classified by the lack of face-to-face communication but connects through a similar school of thought (Anderson 2016).

In the past, community groups have taken form through communal arrangements that may consist of membership requirements, purpose, interactions, and a common factor of bond (Douglas 2010). Membership requirements may include fees, oaths, and previous networking. Online communities may require the same thing through subscription services or previous interaction. There are parallels that can be connected by physical and online communities, but all groups have a common bond that creates a connection with participants. For example, a neighborhood is an example of a physical community. Brint would classify this community as a "Community of Place" (2001, 10).

The common bond in the community of place is geographic. Through geographically focused groups, the barriers that limit the participants would include time, location, and availability of meeting space for members. Neighborhood groups have also evolved as Facebook groups. These geographically tied groups could be created for the households to engage with one another through a platform with very few barriers. These online neighborhood groups provide community and allow members to engage with resources or experiences, such as garbage pickup days, community policing, and events.

Online communities provide a functional space devoid of barriers and provide many gratifications for members who actively seek information for everyday living to help with deeper psychological needs. Understanding online communities must begin with understanding legacy communities. Scholars, such as Tönnies (1957) and Hillery (1955), have categorized legacy communities in different ways, yet their categorizations are helpful in examining the nonlegacy, digital communities created within social platforms. The urban environment and village communities proposed by Tönnies allow the researchers to apply contextualization to the idea of culture and common bonds in social media.

TYPES OF ONLINE COMMUNITIES

As Hillery suggested with social interaction communities, common ties are the leading factors of social interaction communities (1955). Through the common tie of behaviors discussed, online communities create a gathering place for like-minded users (Greene et al. 2011; Lian and Nettleton 2015; Brown and Duguid 2000; Chung 2013; Horst and Miller 2012). The platforms that adequately provide the most popular community options include Facebook, Reddit, and the smartphone app Whisper. While Facebook is identifying with account information, Whisper and Reddit provide anonymity for users. Each platform is a direct representation of Tönnies (1957) Gesellschaft, with the multitude of smaller villages. True to Gesellschaft's nature, online societal culture differs as well. The groups or communities within the Gesellschaft social media platforms represent the Gemeinschaft or the villages of the community.

Facebook

Facebook has different opportunities for users to engage in its platform. Users have individual accounts, which are known as profiles. In personal profiles, users self-identify with their name, profile picture, interests, and location. Profiles have the capability to post status updates through text, photos, videos, and links for their connected friends to see. Through connecting with other personal profiles on Facebook, a newsfeed is created that curates status updates from the connected friends and, in some cases, professional pages. Facebook created pages for organizations, businesses, and influential individuals. This function allows the companies to create a presence to share their own updates, which could range from GIFs, promotions, and other creative elements from the social media team. The goal of posting from the company page would be to create engagement from personal profiles. The users who have created a profile have the capability to like a page, which, in result, would show that page's content on their news feed.

In addition to the engagement between profiles and pages, users can join groups on Facebook. The groups range in a variety of topics that may interest an individual. The researchers do classify the groups as an online community in this research.

Users are able to search for keywords around behaviors such as "depression," and the search results will provide posts, people, photos, pages, and groups that deal with the topic of depression. In a search with the keyword "depression" on Facebook, the platform provided a mixture of pages and groups in the results. However, Facebook has created resources in the first two results on the page.

The first result on Facebook is a shortcut that leads the user to resources for emotional health (figure 3.1). The link leads the user to a mixture of

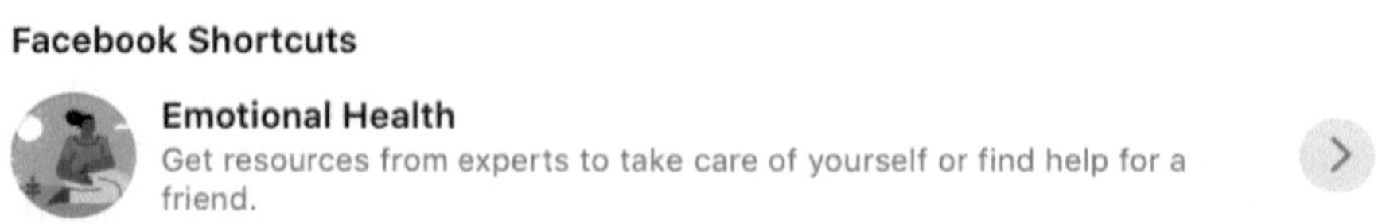

Figure 3.1 Emotional Health Shortcut from Facebook Search Results. *Source*: META. 2021a. Screenshot sourced from https://www.facebook.com/search/top?q=depression. 2021.

informational articles that range from topics. Users are able to read articles about stress, anxiety, emotional crisis, and grief. All available articles are created by reputable organizations that provide resources to the public.

In addition, there are several *calls to action* available on the platform (figure 3.2). Users are encouraged to connect with someone to discuss the emotional experience. At the time of this writing, the contact options include (1) Talk with a friend or (2) Contact a helpline. The helpline options include a mixture of various organizations' phone numbers to call or text or message the helpline on Facebook's native messenger. Users are also given the opportunity to connect with an organization's Facebook pages (figure 3.3). Seeking individuals could either follow or visit the website through the options provided.

On the results page, Facebook provides other resources that are user-based rather than organizationally focused content, as previously mentioned. Groups and pages around the topic of "depression" are provided to the user. On the sidebar of the platform's search results, users can select if they would like to see results of posts, people, photos, videos, marketplace, groups, and

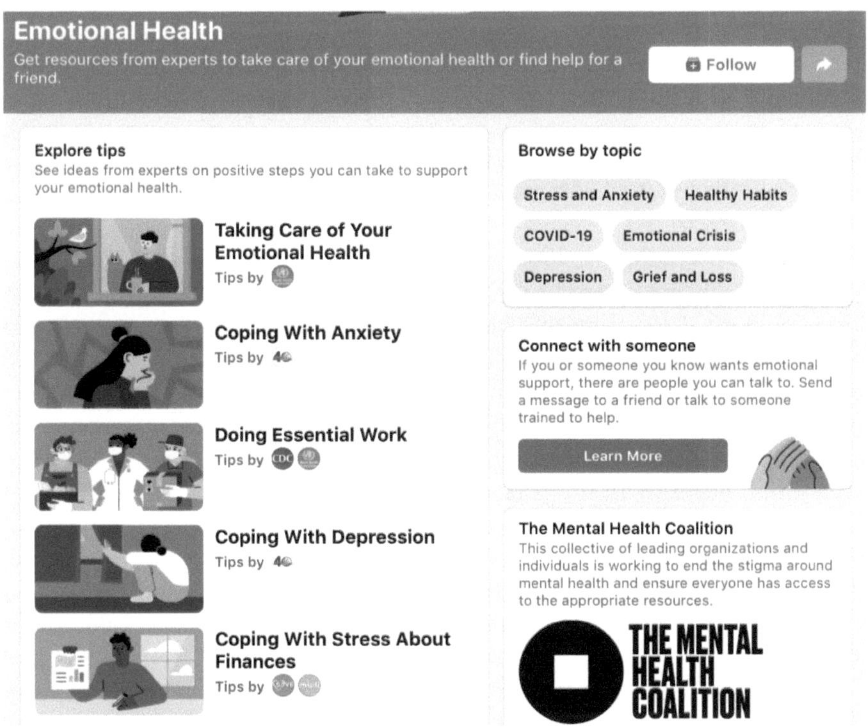

Figure 3.2 Full Availability of Emotional Health Resources on Facebook. *Source*: META. 2021b. Screenshot sourced from https://www.facebook.com/emotional_health. 2021.

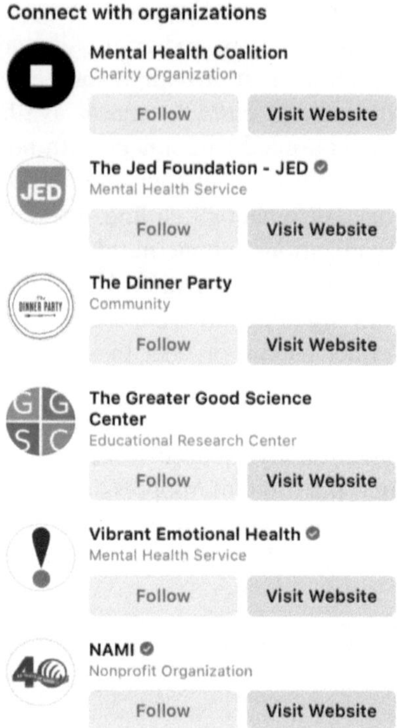

Figure 3.3 Organizations Facebook Provides as Connection Options. *Source*: META. 2021b. Screenshot sourced from https://www.facebook.com/emotional_health. 2021.

so on. Upon selecting the groups under the "depression" results, numerous types of groups are offered to the user. However, on the platform, there is not a categorical structure that allows users to see the most reputable communities or how they are moderated. The platform provides the results in an organizational structure based on group members, groups joined, and other factors Facebook takes into consideration. Each line of the results has the name of the group and the number of members (both inactive and active). Each group has a small information blurb along with an average number of posts a day.

Facebook offers group creation capabilities to every user. Upon the creation of a group, the privacy settings are determined. The group could be a public or private group based on the needs of the community. Public groups allow any user on Facebook to see the posts and comments. Users do not need to be added to the group in order to see the content. Along with the content, all users on Facebook can see the members and the admins of the public group. In a private group, only the members can see the posts and comments posted. The list of private group members can be seen by the members as well. However, the admins of the private group could be viewed by anyone on Facebook (META 2022).

There is a third option for groups that could protect the identities of group members. In addition to the private group privacy settings, Facebook offers a secret group option that is set up as a private group but is undiscoverable by search results. The only way to join these groups would be through an invitation by a current member of the secret group (Binder 2019).

While group options provide online communities for individuals, identities are still revealed through the list of members and the engagement on posts. If the group was classified as a public group, identities would be revealed for all Facebook users to discover. In addition, whether public or private group settings are selected, all moderator identities are revealed for the Facebook group user base. Compared to other platforms, Facebook groups do not offer anonymity for the moderators of the groups. Even in a closed group, the moderators are still available for messaging or connecting through a friend request. However, there are other platforms that provide the anonymity sought in such communities.

Reddit

The social media platform Reddit is based on anonymity and is coined with the phrase "the front page of the Internet." On the platform, Reddit is composed of communities called subreddits, which form the niche communities users can join. In each subreddit, there are rules that help enforce posting guidelines and appropriate content. Moderators have control over posts and comments in every subreddit. The engagements with posts are classified as upvotes and downvotes along with comments and shares. A user can upvote a post or comment if they find it enjoyable and likewise downvote if they disagree. Posts and comments are measured by the voting system. Users are each given a profile with a categorization of all historical posts and comments submitted by said user. The profile shows the cumulative number of upvotes from both posts and comments submitted. Reddit serves as an anonymous platform that is only tied to an email address to log on. The email address is not available for other users to access.

Users can search for subreddits through the search bar at the top of the platform. Upon a search for "depression," the subreddits "r/depression," "r/foreveralone," and "r/depression_help" were the top three communities in the search results (Reddit 2009, 2010c, 2014). Other pieces of content in the search results included posts that mentioned the keyword "depression." The first result was from the subreddit "r/MadeMeSmile" and had two thousand four hundred comments and eighty-six thousand nine hundred upvotes (Reddit 2012a).

Other posts were from "r/pics," "r/Documentaries," and "r/MadeMeSmile" (Reddit 2008a, 2008c, 2012a). The majority of the search results in the posts were discussing post-recoveries and scientific studies around the topic.

The subreddit "r/Depression" was the top result for the keyword "depression" (Reddit 2009). The subreddit provided information on the community: "A supportive space for anyone struggling with depression. FYI, it's usually more helpful to post anything that specifically involves suicidal thoughts or intent in r/SuicideWatch" (Reddit 2008h). If you're concerned about someone else's suicide risk, see their How to Assess Risk page (Reddit 2010a). As mentioned before, each platform has a set of rules for community members to follow. The subreddit r/Depression's rules include these:

1) Text Posts *only*
   - Articles (including personal blogs) and media must be linked in a text submission and accompanied by a full account of your personal experience with them and how they affected your depression.
   - If your resource is of primarily scientific, philosophical, or sociopolitical interest, please post it elsewhere, e.g., r/science, r/philosophy, r/psychology, r/mentalhealth.
   - This also means no fundraising or activism, please.
   - Any surveys or research related posts *must* be pre-approved by the mod team. Approved research posts will have a tag that only moderators can apply.
   - Do not debate or sensationalize current events or hot-button topics because they happen to have a "depression angle."
2) Do not post or respond with
   - "Tough love" of any description.
   - General uplifting or "it gets better" messages. Encouragement is *not* helpful unless it integrates a real personal understanding of the OP's (original poster) feelings and situation.
   - Anything explicit or inciting related to suicide or self-harm.
   - Claims about the efficacy of any treatment or self-help strategy *including religion.*
3) Please do not diagnose others or advocate *for or against* specific treatments or self-help strategies.
   - In response to someone who has asked for help, it is okay to *de*scribe how something worked (or did not) for you, but it is absolutely not okay to *pre*scribe for anybody else.
   - Our focus is on support rather than "fixes." If you are looking for a more solution-oriented community, check out r/GetMotivated / or r/ getting over it/.

4) Do not *say* that you are here to help. *Show* it by responding supportively to our OPs.
   - Empathy, support, and feedback are usually more helpful than advice.
   - Do not advertise yourself as a helper, authority, or role model. This includes inviting private messages as a first resort.
   - If you struggle with knowing how best to empathize and connect with others, this brief video from Brené Brown and the RSA may help.
   - You do not need special knowledge or expertise to help; you just need to be nonjudgmental and interested in understanding the other person's experience. (Reddit 2006, 2008, 2008b, 2008e, 2009, 2010, 2010b; Brown et al. 2013).

Below the listed rules, the community does offer additional resources for the user. The resources state:

> We are not a crisis service. We can't guarantee an immediate response, and there are times when this subreddit is relatively quiet. This does not mean no one cares. If you need to talk to someone at once, you may want to take a look at our Hotline Numbers. (2008i)

In the same text box, other subreddits: r/anxiety, r/ADHD, r/BipolarReddit, and r/stopselfharm are shared for possible connection and engagement for the users (Reddit 2008f, 2008g, 2009b, 2011). The final sidebar option includes an opportunity for the user to message the moderators. A large button is in the design to message all moderators, or users could select the moderator they want to message out of a list displaying all usernames and profiles of the moderators.

The categorization of posts is based on the voting system on the Reddit platform. As posts are upvoted, they rise in popularity. In comparison, the downvoted posts decrease not only in popularity but also in the ranking on the page. At the top of the posts submitted, users could rank from "Hot," "New," and "Top" (figure 3.4). The "Hot" category showcases the most popular posts at that time. "New" displays the newest submissions in chronological order. While "Top" gives the user an option to see the most popular posts of that current time, that day, the week, month, year, and all-time.

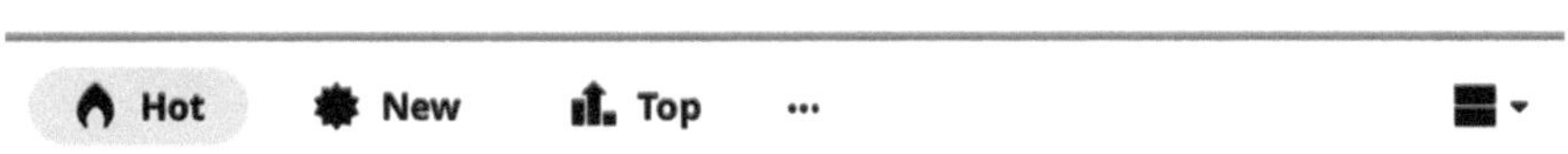

Figure 3.4 Reddit Toolbar—Sorts and Filters Posts Based on Hot, New, or Top Classification. *Source*: Screenshot sourced from https://www.reddit.com. 2021.

Whisper

The app available on Google Play and Apple App Store "Whisper" deems itself as a community where users can unite under anonymity (figure 3.5).

> Ever wondered [*sic*] what the people around you are really thinking? Whisper is an online community where millions of people around the world share real thoughts, trade advice, and get the inside scoop.
>
> "The experience of spending time on Whisper is unlike any other major social network: It's more raw, more moving . . . and yes, often more addictive." —Mashable
>
> Chat directly with other Whisper users—it is a great way to meet new people. Join the thirty million+ people who use Whisper every month; it will change the way you see the world. (Apple 2022)

Figure 3.5 Whisper—App Description from Apple's App Store. *Source*: Screenshot sourced from Apple. https://apps.apple.com/us/app/whisper-share-express-meet/id506141837. 2021.

While the platform is not the typical mainstream social media platform, the researchers do classify it as an online community. Upon joining, users can join groups that appeal to their own interests. The platform is based on the ability to share a statement in an anonymous way. The app states, "Express yourself openly and honestly" (Apple 2022). The user design of the application includes four tabs for users to select to find the statements or as the application has coined the phrase: "Whispers."

Users can "Find a group" and search for keywords determined by their own interests or, in this case, behavior. There are endless groups focused on the commonality of depression, suicide, anxiety, and more. While groups may be more active than others, the ranking is based on the number of members in the search results.

The popular option allows users to see the most interacted whispers at that time. *Nearby* uses the self-identifying location on the users' smartphones to allow nearby users to see the whispers in their area. With the latest tab, the most recent whispers are displayed on the screen. Users can engage with the whispers through commenting back with a whisper, sharing the whisper, or messaging the original poster. The chat function allows communication between each user based on individual whispers. Users cannot see the full list of whispers other users posted, which provides a stronger sense of anonymity. However, users are given a nickname that they can change at any time with no time limits in between.

ONLINE SOCIAL GROUPS

In the last decade, technology has evolved in a way where people can communicate with each other with ease through different platforms. This could take place through a newsletter, online communication, or chat rooms, and it eventually led up to the creation of the first social media site in 1997: Six Degrees (Ngak 2011). In this platform, users could create a profile, as they built their following, and meet individuals online. As this site developed, other platforms were discovered, such as LinkedIn's precursor Ryze in 2001 and Friendster in 2002. In 2003, Myspace provided a place where people could share blogs, comment on profiles, and share music—where it surpassed Yahoo! in total page views in November 2006 (Arrington 2006).

LinkedIn then started developing as a commonplace to network with business professionals that was eventually purchased by Microsoft for $26 billion (Ngak 2011; Novet 2019). In 2004, a network was launched that changed how the world views online communities. Mark Zuckerberg created "The Facebook" as an undergraduate at Harvard University—two years later, Facebook expanded to any user who had an email address (Phillips 2013).

Facebook facilitated an opportunity for students to join an online community through the common bond of the university. Through this platform, they were able to connect with others in their local proximity, based on the educational institutions they have attended. In the "2012 Quarter 3 Investor Report," Facebook stated that they had reached one billion users, while at the end of 2020, Facebook reached 2.79 billion monthly users (Iqbal 2021). Platform users can take advantage of several of the functions that Facebook has to offer, including private, closed, and open groups. In September 2016, it was found that eight hundred fifty million people were active in Facebook groups (Guynn 2016). While technology evolves, there will always be a basic need for community. The culture will then adapt to what technology is available to fulfill the gratifications sought from the individual.

Instagram has two billion monthly active users (Chen 2022) and anonymous communities are just as large. The online platform Reddit is the sixth most visited site in the United States (Alexa Internet, Inc. 2022). Reddit has over one hundred thirty-eight thousand online communities. Each community is known as a *subreddit*, which is monitored by one or a team of moderators to ensure the quality of postings and topics. While this site has impressive numbers, the length of engagement is even more astonishing. "The average user spends 15 minutes 47 seconds on Reddit.com each day, compared to just over 11 minutes for visitors to Facebook.com, and 6 minutes 23 seconds on Twitter.com" (Kemp 2018, para. 6).

While these statistics are important to consider, Reddit provides an entirely different type of community than Facebook on the basis of providing anonymity to the user base. According to Gutman, Reddit's co-founder Steve Huffman

> argued that anonymity on Reddit actually makes using the site "more like a conversation one has in real life" than other exchanges on the Internet. When people detach from their real-world identities, they can be more authentic, more true to themselves. (2018, para. 3)

Though Reddit has a large engagement on their anonymous platform, Facebook also provides an online community, but with identity revealing data through the user profiles. Through the Facebook platform, over 400 million users are involved in groups that Facebook has classified as meaningful. The groups include a variety of topics ranging from new parenting and mental health to disease diagnosis support (Rodriguez 2020).

Support groups have evolved from physical meetings to online communities in the past couple of years. Online groups are catered to the individualized needs of the person. As people have various therapeutic needs, physical presence and face-to-face interaction could be determining factors in selecting a form of therapy. Users may value anonymity and feel like they can share more freely, thus resulting in higher trust in the online community (Lobchuk et al. 2015). The face-to-face community could create a barrier for participants if they do not have the previous connections of a bond. However, there are platform functions that would help users become better acquainted with other members. Online groups have evolved from the back-and-forth exchange of messages (AOL, Yahoo! Messenger) to social media platforms with numerous modalities of communication such as messages, comments, and shares.

Users are also able to provide a sense of their own self-identity through the customization of the profile. Various platforms allow profile pictures, cover photos, layout, content, avatars, and image frames to all be customized to reflect the personality or affinity interests of the users. With the customization options that are available to users of all platforms, communities provide insight into who is involved with the group. This would also allow moderators or administrators of the groups to verify members through an approval process to continually provide a healthy community. With the expansion of information through technological advancements, access to medical treatment and communication allows users to have more trust and ownership of their well-being (Hesse et al. 2005; Medlock et al. 2015; Swan 2012). In previous research, it was found that online communities could provide support for users (Zhang et al. 2017; Kingod et al. 2017). These online groups allow users to gain support from others who are going through the same stages of life or diagnosis.

Online Groups as Therapy

While physical support groups could be beneficial, they do not always provide the support one may need if diagnosed with chronic illness (Bury 1982; Corbin and Strauss 1987; Nielsen and Grøn 2012; Strauss and Glaser 1975). Online groups, however, eliminate barriers to participation that are present in physical support therapy. In a physical setting, group members must drive to therapy, which can be difficult for people diagnosed with PTSD or other phobias (Bouchard et al. 2004). Past studies of online communities have supported positive outcomes, such as reduced depression and increased social support (Lieberman et al. 2003; Børøsund et al. 2014; Winzelberg et al. 2003; Gustafson et al. 2001; Smith et al. 2021).

Previous studies of online health communities have focused on social support, member characteristics, content, the impact of participation, and engagement of the user (Zhang et al. 2017). Bourdieu classified these concepts as the cultural and social capital of communities (1986, 241–58). Culture influences the member characteristics that users have adopted or inherited from their upbringing. The social capital explains the interactions between the members of a high bond community. The bond connects users who have similar characteristics. Zhang (2017) determined that the type, source, and setting of the support are important to understand when researching the communities. To further understand the benefits of health-focused communities, an analysis of the current research can provide a valuable perspective. Chen and Xu suggested that among online communities, the members "play the role of not only recipients but also providers of social support in online communities. Their willingness to provide social support is essential for the development and success of online communities" (2021, 1).

Previous studies have found the benefits of online support groups in connecting with individuals with similar illnesses (Chen and Xu 2021; Greene et al. 2011; Lian and Nettleton 2015; Brown and Duguid 2000; Chung 2013; Horst and Miller 2012). Through a qualitative analysis of previously published articles that discussed online peer-to-peer communities and chronic illness, researcher Kingod et al. (2017) coded four main themes discussed from thirteen articles. Researchers found that four main themes of the qualitative data included "(a) illness-associated identity work, (b) social support and connectivity, (c) experiential knowledge sharing, and (d) collective voice and mobilization" (Kingod et al. 2017). The top sub-themes in the research were solidarity and exchange of experience. Both sub-themes were found in the majority of articles studied (Kingod et al. 2017). Solidarity and exchange of experience have not only been used for "illness-associated groups" but online communities based on experiences, such as the COVID-19 pandemic.

Online communities have been found to provide support for cancer survivors. Walsh and Al Achkar studied lung cancer support groups to determine the type of engagement the users primarily acted upon. Several users in the study were absent from engagement and lurked in the community. This could be due to a "preference for reading about others' experiences (versus sharing their own), worsening health (e.g., disease progression), or competing life demands (e.g., caregiving responsibilities)" (2021, 6). Past negative experiences could also be a determining factor for the lack of engagement.

Walsh and Al Achkar (2021) also found that community members were interested in finding past experiences, resources, and information from other peers. Through the engagement between peers, lung cancer survivors were able to provide support through their own lived experience, which in turn, would answer the emotional questions presented by diagnosed individuals. The openness of lived experiences was also shared in similar online health communities that provided emotional support for participants (Kingod et al. 2017). However, the trajectory of behavior modification falls solely on the user's gratification and acceptance of the current reality.

Online Stroke Communities

Support continues to be a primary factor in the engagement with online communities. While support can help individuals process feelings of their behaviors or condition, acceptance of reality is dependent on the user. Smith et al. (2021) described this concept through the understanding of stroke survivors in online communities. The research team found that the major themes of posts in stroke-focused communities were the following: prayer/well-wishing, suggestions/advice, understanding/empathy, validation, and encouragement (Smith et al. 2021).

Along with the qualitative thematic analysis, Smith et al. (2021) created two trajectories for the user experience. After the stroke event, the user decided on the adjustment of the new reality. Users were placed on the positive emotional adjustment trajectory through support from family and friends, joining groups, starting hobbies, interacting with others, online or in person peer support, and emotional therapy. The positive adjustment provides cheerfulness, positive attitudes, gratefulness, relief, and determination. The three phases of immediate, intermediate, and final stages lead to "eventual complete acceptance of stroke and 'new self'" (Smith et al. 2021, 420). Stroke survivors were engaged in negative emotional adjustments through the end of physio, changes to living arrangements, negative reactions, and a lack of emotional aftercare. This led the survivor into depression, anger, guilt, isolation and the ongoing thought of "inability to accept stroke or 'new self,' depression" (Smith et al. 2021, 420).

According to Smith et al. (2021), the survivors could transition from one trajectory to another upon any interaction with positive or negative events. For example, joining an online support group would assist the survivor in accomplishing the need for acceptance of the stroke and their "new self." Though the acceptance of one's reality is dependent on the individual, medical professionals could implement professional therapy in online communities in their practice.

Videoconferencing

Professional therapy has been attempted through online communication, but several barriers were found. Videoconferencing has proven to be an effective communication tool regarding telehealth (Guaiana et al. 2021). In an analysis of videoconferencing psychotherapy, researchers found that clinician attitudes were the most common barrier. However, the professionals that have had previous experience with videoconferencing psychotherapy facilitated the adoption of the technology in their practice.

Adoption of the videoconferencing tools was accepted more if the medical office had staff dedicated to the technology. Due to the online nature of the therapy, connectivity to the Internet was required (Guaiana et al. 2021). Connectivity continues to be a limitation to involvement in online communities from a user's perspective. If medical professionals were to include online communities in treatment, training and additional staff would be required to become effective.

In a study by Nelson, Bernard, and Cain (2003), the researchers found that children exposed to videoconferencing formats for mental health interventions had a reduction in depression, and it took fewer sessions for that reduction to occur than those in more traditional interventions.

Slone, Reese, and McClellan's 2012 extensive review of telepsychology outcomes for children and teens called for greater exploration into mental health care via mediums such as the Internet, videoconferencing, and phone. They called on researchers to explore a multitude of interventions to help people dealing with mental health issues. They especially suggested a need for studies in more rural and remote areas, similar to those that are the focus of the present research.

COVID-19

During the coronavirus pandemic, users developed their perceptions of the virus and preventive measures based on media consumption. Igartua, Ortega-Mohedano, and Arcila-Calderón's 2020 cross-cultural study, using an online survey of participants in twenty-six countries, was conducted to better understand how people use media to gather information related to health. In the midst of the first months of the coronavirus, the researchers worked to better understand how media content and the format of that content impacted engagement with audiences. Among the 750-plus participants, the majority were from Spain, China, Brazil, Italy, Ecuador, the United States, and Mexico—countries where information may be readily available and two countries where it may not be easily accessible. Media consumption in this study included websites visited, social media platforms, face-to-face conversations, and legacy media such as TV, radio, newspaper, and magazines. While users may seek out information, researchers found that accessibility to media was limited. And, noteworthy was that while the legacy media were identified as one single latent dimension, social media were not. Instead, Igartua, Ortega-Mohedano, and Arcila-Calderón (2020) found that while legacy media is a single latent dimension impacting knowledge consumption, social media is divided between those sites that contain a great visual component engaged with "likes" on social media platforms (Facebook, Instagram, and YouTube) and platforms that rely on text (Twitter and Reddit) that possess more of a conversational element such as what is offered with WhatsApp. Data from the study showed that contact on social media may be different between the different categories and formats of social media platforms. Likewise, the researchers found gender and age related to the type of media platform used with both legacy media and social media. While the visual social posts included visual components such as YouTube and TikTok videos, written posts were descriptive information such as Tweets and Reddit text posts (Igartua Ortega-Mohedano, and Arcila-Calderón 2020). Igartua, Ortega-Mohedano, and Arcila-Calderón suggested descriptive information including "'written-dialogical' social media"; in other words, written dialogue, much like a text message, yet within a group, impacts the gathering of health information (2020, 11).

In online communities focused on self-damaging behaviors, text posts are the primary type of posting. Several communities have a ban on videos or images to mitigate triggering image risks. For example, the subreddit rules for r/f—keatingdisorders include these: "1. No photos; 2. No pro-ana/mia content; 3. No medical advice; 10. No diet tips; 11. Research/Survey approval" (Reddit 2014a). The admins create the rules to protect the community and prevent toxicity or risks of behavioral actions. While admins are creating a safe community, the users provide a sense of support through engagement.

Social Support

Greidanus and Everall wrote, "The Internet provides individuals with the opportunity to connect with others in a community created around similar concerns with others who can provide both information and emotional support" (2010, 193). Greidanus and Everall also suggested that "social networks are the fabric of communities" and within online communities exist mutual self-help members (2010, 193). Members serve as peer support for one another. Greidanus and Everall's online mutual help groups are different from physical support groups because the messages are "generally asynchronous," meaning individuals may take as much time as they wish in composing their messages, and responses to messages, and a "greater emphasis is placed on the authors' choices of words and the readers' interpretations when determining the meaning of a message" (2010, 193–4). Greidanus and Everall's (2010) content analysis of posted message transcripts left within online therapy communities for those dealing with suicidal tendencies showed there were help seekers in the community, trained volunteers, and help providers. The original help seeker was found to be able to engage with the community and ultimately became a help provider while still remaining a help seeker. They found with the give-and-take of communication within the group that a safe community was created where members felt like they could share information about themselves and their relationships. In many cases of this study, the members were dealing with suicidal thoughts and self-damaging behaviors.

In this study, the discussion of suicide, most often centered on life events, was a trigger for feeling a lack of purpose. The trained volunteers provided messages that thoughts of self-damaging behaviors were "understandable" in situations where life events impacted feelings of purpose or lack thereof. In this case, the volunteers encouraged people to seek available resources to get professional help. The help provider served in a different capacity, encouraging the help seekers to write more about their situations and to show the help seekers that the online therapy community cared about them while showing empathy, empowerment, and concern. Often the help provider would encourage the help seekers to write about their source of purpose and their hopes for the future. What was seen over time within the context of the written post was that

> members often expressed emotional support by telling a story of how they had similar feelings at one time in their lives. These types of responses are of particular interest when the community member had initially been a help seeker. Their messages usually conveyed empathy and encouraged continued participation in the community. In this way, those who began as help seekers grew into new roles as help providers. (Greidanus and Everall 2010, 199)

The community developed when help seekers felt understood by the online therapy members. The feeling of community "appeared to be especially strong for those help seekers who felt misunderstood by those in their 'offline' lives" (Greidanus and Everall 2010, 199). Participants in this study enjoyed the engagement they shared with other members of the online therapy community. A suggestion from their work is that there are two kinds of community—locational and relational. The online community thrives as a relational community where support is provided through empathetic support, and the community is willing to be helped by both seekers and help providers.

Chen and Xu's 2021 content analyzed the mental health subreddit communities to better understand how communities that provided social support impacted members compared to those communities that appeared to provide less support. Additionally, they looked closely at the content of the social support posts to determine the degree of empathy. What they found was that if a person's initial post received empathetic support upon the post being published, the member receiving that support would be more likely to provide empathetic support to other postings and members. Chen and Xu (2021) concluded that positive engagement with other members was "contagious" and would make the community more supportive in the eyes of the member. Thus, if an individual received engagement in their initial experiences with the online community, the individual was likely to be more engaged with other users and be more emphathetic toward new users.

Online Mental Health Services

Dunbar et al. (2018) used a survey to learn more about how community college students perceived online mental health services. The researchers surveyed more than 6,000 respondents. Among the participants, 28 percent of students reported in person mental health treatments, but only 3 percent indicated they had used online services. Yet, among those responding, 60 percent indicated they would be willing to use online services. Respondents indicated that online therapy would reduce travel issues and online therapy could be provided at convenient times. While the focus in these cases was individual treatment, group treatment options may well benefit an online therapy community member. Taking the first step to getting treatment is often hard. Students who had already participated in, in person treatment indicated they would prefer in person over online therapy, while those with no prior experience with in person mental health treatment were hesitant to seek helpful treatment in person or online. Notably, participants with past treatment or no treatment at all were equally willing to use online treatment services. Dunbar et al. concluded that "online services may hold promise as a first contact point with mental health treatment (for example, as part of a screening and triage system or a gateway to more intensive in person treatment) and as a means of addressing unmet treatment need among individuals with no previous experience of in person treatment (that is, most students with treatment need)" (Williams et al. 2014, as cited by Dunbar et al. 2018, 599). Likewise, we believe online therapy communities may serve as a means to help individuals with mental health issues and serve as a first step in reaching out for professional help.

Lal and Adair's 2014 review of e-mental health literature showed that online therapies may be useful in helping people deal with some forms of mental health issues. They found in their review of one hundred and fifteen studies that social support comes in many formats, including discussion groups, bulletin boards, chat rooms, blogs, and social media. Likewise, Lal and Adair suggested online therapy communities may be "particularly promising for rural and remote populations. They are also promising for subpopulations that have other barriers to access (attitudinal, financial, or temporal) or that avoid treatment because of stigma" (2014, para. 17). Lal and Adair's 2014 extensive review of literature called for more work in studying the value of online therapy communities and other e-interventions that may help individuals with self-harming behaviors.

Likewise, Slone, Reese, and McClellan (2012) called for more research into telepsychology counseling after their extensive review of the literature with a focus on youth and telepsychology. They wrote the literature suggested that telepsychology works better than no treatment at all. But they believed that the literature showed the lack of a strong methodological approach in studies conducted thus far. They believed that research needed to be conducted within rural and diverse regions, using a variety of research models. To that end, this research was designed using two methodological approaches to better understand online community therapy groups: a qualitative approach using in-depth interviews and a quantitative survey. The survey was introduced to rural populations in North and South Carolina and Arkansas.

Self-Harming Forums

Eichenberg and Schott (2017) conducted a survey of 300-plus adolescents living in Germany. Among the respondents, most had participated in self-harming forums for just a little less than two years. Most visited the forums at least once a day. Respondents indicated there were three main reasons why the participants visited the forums throughout the day: (1) to meet people who were dealing with the same kinds of problems, (2) to share problems with others, and (3) to be able to help other people. Less prevalent among the motivations was to gather information or ask for help, and less likely to express urges to self-harm. Respondents were not looking for ways to learn new techniques of self-harming.

Rodham, Gavin, and Miles (2007), in their qualitative study just prior to the explosion of the social media platforms, noted that support groups helped people to have a sense of hope, belonging, and an opportunity to express themselves. Online therapy groups are an extension of support groups, and the outcome is often similar with members finding hope, belonging, and free expression. They suggested from their content analysis of a self-help message board and associated posts followed an overall theme of support from the online support group where participants sought validation of self-worth, crisis support, and a place to express feelings. Rodham, Gavin, and Miles concluded that online message boards provide members with "a safe environment where they could talk about things they found difficult to talk about in face-to-face encounters" (2007, 428). They did suggest that this support could be undermined by message board members who may not be trained professionals, which could impact the effect of interactions within the community. They also called for in-depth interviews and surveys to be used to better understand the uses and gratifications obtained within online communities as people seek to be heard and supported (Rodham, Gavin, and Miles 2007).

Scholars in psychology, sociology, and health professions have studied the impact of support communities for people who exhibit self-harming behaviors (Smith et al. 2021; Chen and Xu 2021; Walsh and Al Achkar 2021; Lal and Adair 2014; Lian and Nettleton 2015; Chung 2013; Horst and Miller 2012; Greene et al. 2011; Brown and Duguid 2000). Yet, the lenses used do not consider theoretical approaches in mass communication, which examine the symbiotic relationship of online therapy group members as they use social media platforms to connect to like positioned individuals who struggle with self-harming behaviors.

Chapter 4

Theoretical Approaches to Communities

Using a mass communication approach to examine online communities is relevant as the researchers explore the impact of gratifications on the use and engagement with online therapy groups. McLuhan (1964) suggested that a symbiotic relationship exists between message content and the medium in which that message is transmitted. A better understanding of online platforms for communities and the content and support found there may lead to more robust engagement with members of online groups which may be useful in leading individuals away from self-harming behaviors. The online community can meet the needs of the members by providing social support (Norman et al. 2008) and support that shows empathy toward newer members of the group. Initial engagement with a first-time member's post leads a new member to find the group more welcoming and increases the willingness to engage with others who are seeking help (Chen and Xu 2021). Much like walking into a physical room and engaging with others, the online group that interacts with a member's posts becomes a much safer place to engage and receive support and might steer the member away from self-harming behaviors. Examining the uses of online therapy communities and gratifications obtained from that interaction allows the researchers to look beyond the traditional theories and interventions used to explore mental health issues (Bell 2007; Ybarra and Eaton 2005; Ruggiero 2000). Bell suggested (2007) that people glean a great deal of information from online sources. Evaluating the sources of information is increasingly difficult because of the magnitude of the sources that provide some information about mental health. Bell (2007) suggested online groups may allow the users to express themselves more freely, and mental health providers may be able to reframe what might traditionally be framed as a "mental disorder" into a more positive frame.

Ybarra and Eaton (2005) explored Internet interventions and looked at what they called the more passive interventions (educational websites and online mental health screenings) and then examined online therapy and support groups. They called for health professionals to use the Internet to reach those challenged by accessibility,

> utilizing this new technology, mental health professionals can provide evidence-based interventions and prevention programs to numbers of people that before would have been financially unfeasible. The Internet reaches people who have traditional access issues, including those in rural areas without local providers, as well as those who are loath to seek treatment because they prize their privacy. (Ybarra and Eaton 2005, 84)

Ruggiero suggested within the context of the uses and gratifications theory, "The basic questions remain the same. Why do people become involved in one particular type of mediated communication or another, and what gratifications do they receive from it?" (2000, 29). Ruggiero also suggested as we were moving into the twenty-first century that the uses and gratifications theory must develop to address "interactivity, demassification, hypertextuality, asynchronicity, and interpersonal aspects of mediated communication" (2000, 29).

Because of the changing media ecology and the ability to have interactivity in online therapy communities, research is needed to understand the interactions among community members and how these interactions are perceived, used, and valued. Whether professionally led online therapy communities or member-led therapy communities, the ability to connect regardless of geographic location provides individuals who experience self-damaging behaviors the opportunity to learn from one another and to receive and provide support to community members. Bell (2007), Ybarra and Eaton (2005), and Ruggiero (2000) called for new methodological approaches to studying online therapy communities. For this reason, we approach the current research from the uses and gratifications perspective and examine closely the importance of community, interactivity, and support using a two-pronged methodological strategy—qualitative interviews and surveys.

USES AND GRATIFICATIONS THEORY

To better understand communities, one must approach the study of communities with a theoretical lens. While many may use sociological and psychological theories when studying online therapy groups, the researchers believe the uses and gratifications theory can be useful in explaining audience behaviors toward the various online therapy groups. The goal of this theory is to understand what gratifications the receiver desires from communication and the community and its members. Katz, Blumler, and Gurevitch (1973) would suggest understanding the motives people have toward media and the gratifications from using media content and experiencing engagement, all lend themselves to finding ways to use media content to help others live life. Ruggiero (2000) argued that the uses and gratifications theory provides flexibility where "computer-mediated communication permeates every aspect of our individual and social lives" (2000, 28). No matter the media platform, Ruggiero (2000) suggested the overarching purpose of uses and gratifications lies with why people use one platform over another and what gratifications exist for users. Online therapy groups allow for interactions not impacted by geographic location. Those seeking help through online therapy groups are considered to be active audience members, who are seeking engagement with other members.

Katz, Blumler, and Gurevitch (1973) suggested that to understand how people use media platforms, you must recognize that the audience actively seeks information, tends to be goal oriented, is intentionally seeking to fulfill a need, and can recount how some media platforms over another media platform can fulfill a need more fully than other platforms. Audience members and group members can assess the value of any given platform in addressing a need among the users. Blumler (1979) went on to say that people's motivations intentionally impacted the audience's participation, engagement, and consumption of content within online therapy groups. Further, one can distinguish among users between activeness and activity. Where activity would refer to what the audience member does with media content, and activeness refers to the level of engagement where the audience member has the autonomy to participate and engage with the group at different levels of involvement at different times.

Katz, Haas, and Gurevitch (1973) suggested that there are categories of needs, impacting how media content is used by the members of an online group. Online therapy community members may seek out therapy groups to acquire information or knowledge (cognitive needs), increase feelings of belonging or support (affective needs), improve credibility or status (personal integrative needs), interact with group members (social integrative needs), and for escape or diversion (tension release). Lin wrote,

> the uses and gratifications perspective is a bona fide home-grown communication theory with intrinsic social-psychological roots. Although not without criticism from certain scholars, the uses and gratifications perspective has proven to be an axiomatic theory in that it is readily applicable to wide-ranging situations involving mediated communication. Succinctly put, the strength of this theory is its ability to allow researchers to study mediated communication situations via a single or multiple sets of psychological needs, psychological motives,

> communication channels, communication content, and psychological gratifications within a particular or cross-cultural context. (1996, para. 1)

Using this theory in regard to the topic of online community groups as a complementary therapy would support the gratifications that users seek out, not only in a group setting but also in an online setting as well. Using the three objectives, one can conclude that users who seek out support groups are seeking a way for media to gratify their needs. The motives behind seeking an online group and interacting are to find freedom or support from the damaging behavior in the individual. As users follow through seeking and engaging, the following functions of higher self-esteem, more engagement in the public world, or acceptance of oneself could happen when gratifications are met. An example can be seen in Wenner, Palmgreen, and Rosengren's discussion: "If a person values information about current issues and events positively and believes (expects) that television news possesses such information, he or she will be motivated to seek such information from the television news" (1985, 22). On the topic at hand, if an online user thinks that a support group will provide positive gratification, he or she will seek out that type of communication medium to experience that positive experience. Several types of gratifications sought do rely on the user's actions, and whether individuals will actively pursue the desired result (Wenner, Palmgreen, and Rosengren 1985). In this case, different social media users have different gratifications they seek, depending on the case of the damaging behavior. While a percentage of the audience may seek the gratification of high self-esteem from the support group medium, others may pursue the gratification of finding a place of belonging.

Regarding the topic of using online groups in a therapeutic manner, individuals may find media as an alternative to interacting with the physical world (Gerbner et al. 2002). This allows users who may find it difficult to engage with people in a physical setting to have the ability to become more open online. Breaking this topic into the four segments of the framework, the research showed that the sender, message, medium, and receiver flow did not work when compared to the uses and gratifications theory. The researchers believe that for the topic this flow should be reversed, as it is the receiver searching for the communication gratifications that they are seeking. The receiver is not contributing to communication content; rather, they are seeking out mediums for a message sent by a sender. As a receiver searches for the medium of an online group, they are searching for support in a specific venue where they can find gratification. In the medium, the receiver finds the message that references the gratification, whether that message is support or a resource. The message was initially sent from the sender as a "post" or "comment" that has accomplished the gratification sought by the receiver.

Greenberg's 1974 Work on Uses and Gratifications Theory

Greenberg's (1974) work on the uses and gratification theory provided interesting results in the framing for this topic. In order to identify the uses and gratifications, Greenberg conducted a survey among 726 young people, nine to fifteen years old in London, England. During this questionnaire, Greenberg wanted to know why these children watched television. The results of the 180 essays that were completed concluded that there were eight reasons that this audience spent time watching TV: "(1) To pass time; (2) to forget, as a means of diversion; (3) to learn about things; (4) to learn about myself; (5) for arousal; (6) for relaxation; (7) for companionship; and (8) as a habit" (Greenberg 1974, 73–4). These results were organized into a questionnaire, which finalized the core viewing gratifications to six motivations: (1) as a habit, (2) for arousal, (3) for companionship, (4) to relax, (5) to forget, and (6) to pass time (Greenberg 1974, 77).

Notably, the schoolchildren who were given both the essay and the questionnaire did not use the terms "entertainment" or "information." When placed in comparison to the topic at hand, social media could provide entertainment for a user; however, the researcher believes that the main gratifications are more inner-self-focused, similar to the results of Greenberg's study. There are no external impacts on the uses of television in this research; however, it can be gathered that self-pleasure is the overarching motivator over the eight uses. When placed in the research of community groups, the research could safely take all eight uses as a research basis of the uses and gratifications of online community group engagement with individuals who exhibit self-harming tendencies. Greenberg (1974) concluded that different types of media provide different gratifications. For example, self-help social media groups may provide a different gratification than a self-help video.

Mark R. Levy and Sven Windahl on the Concept of Audience Activity

As presented earlier, the uses and gratifications theory is not just one theory, but multiple theories under one central concept (Blumler 1979). This provides several different perspectives regarding this theory. In addition to the uses and gratifications theory, the researchers found it important to apply McQuail and Gurevitch's 1974 "three types of perspectives" to the concept of audience activity: "The functional, which has a 'needs-gratifications' focus; the structural-cultural, which emphasizes the social regulation of both media content and exposure behaviors; and the action/motivation, which stresses the individual as a purposive actor" (Levy and Windahl 1985, 111).

As the topic is placed in McQuail and Gurevitch's (1974) audience activity framework, the researchers could understand the actions or motivations perspective of the research. In addition to the proposed goals of bond, hope, trust, and self-confidence, other motivations may occur based on intrinsic motivations. The audience activity perspective may allow the gratification seeker to act within a community to "kill time" and "may freely interpret the messages received as trivial or involving" (Levy and Windahl 1985, 111). While the action of seeking information in online community content is important, the gratification relies on the receiver's action steps, "an almost boundless freedom to engage in the so-called projected act" (Levy and Windahl 1985, 111). As a result, the responsibility of providing gratification is transferred from the receiver to the community. As this perspective meets the psychological and social needs of online members, understanding the audience activity perspective is important. It would eventually determine the needs of the individual (Levy and Windahl 1985).

For example, by applying the functional perspective, gratification is placed as the responsibility of the platform. This would place the gratifications of communal bond, hope, trust, and self-confidence goals as community expectations. This perspective would place a large responsibility on not only the communities but the social media platforms themselves. However, platforms cannot provide everything that an individual desires regarding the gratifications sought. Due to external factors in users' lives, eliminating the actors' responsibility for platform-met gratifications cannot be accomplished.

In addition, an individual may seek (act) for a sense of communal bond or hope in the online community. Through the action/motivation perspective in the audience activity framework, the gratification relies solely on the individual as they pursue an intrinsic motivation. While this concept is individualistic by nature, it does not consider the engagement with other members who are also contributing through comments and messages in the community.

The researchers propose a unique blend of audience activity concepts that do not hold the platforms responsible for gratifications but become that transport device between two receivers engaging in acts that pursue the same goals. This eliminates the responsibility from the platforms and allows the actors to become providers and receivers through the collaboration community.

While the other perspectives (action/motivation and functional perspectives) work within the research, the structural/cultural perspective does not align with this topic (Levy and Windahl 1985). This perspective proposes limitations across socioeconomic lines, meaning technology and access to certain types of media could be different for different subgroups of people (Levy and Windahl 1985). While limitations exist, the structural/cultural perspective discusses the inequality of digital accessibility across society. While certain households may have access to the Internet and online communities, factors such as income, Internet accessibility, time, culture, and upbringing may limit the opportunities for online involvement.

How Online Communities Are Involved with the Uses and Gratifications Theory

As culture shifts into the connected world that we see today, the health-care system has adopted several new methods to keep up with tech-savvy patients. Medical care is no longer unidirectional, but rather patients are informed by resources provided by community members and Internet search results. It has previously been estimated that two-thirds of adults who have an online presence have used digital resources to understand and discover medical information (Hesse et al. 2005). In Hesse et al.'s 2005 results, the majority of adults who searched online for medical information were over the age of sixty-five. Informative gratifications are sought through using online medical resources. While informative gratifications may be fulfilled through resource discovery, gratifications of communal bond and trust are sought higher through online community platforms. Researching online provides a variety of sources about any given topic the user desires to search. In order to fully understand the flow of uses and gratifications sought when searching online, the researchers propose an online community search pathway that they believe users move through.

As an individual is impacted by the behaviors mentioned in this book, digital means may be used for an answer regarding the said situations. Users then move into the pathway of seeking advice digitally. Digital resources can consist of two methods: (1) users use a search engine (Google, Yahoo, etc.) and are given a search engine results page (SERP) or (2) community platforms are used to search for groups that are focused around certain behaviors. While the SERP provides a mixture of websites and community platforms on occasion, it is not a reliable source of online community discovery. Google results consider different factors determining the results for the search terms used in the search query. This could eliminate communities from being ranked on the top page of the SERP and deliver informative resources from organizations (figure 4.1).

Alternatively, users may type in behavioral keywords such as *depression* or *suicide* on community platforms (Reddit, Facebook, forums, etc.). Upon searching for the keyword, the user will find communities that focus on the behaviors. While joining groups, users initially experience the gratification of communal bond (Chen and Xu 2021). This specific gratification is met through the bond of shared experiences and behaviors of other members. However, the researchers believe that there are three other types of gratifications sought when interaction occurs in the group: (1) hope of recovery, (2)

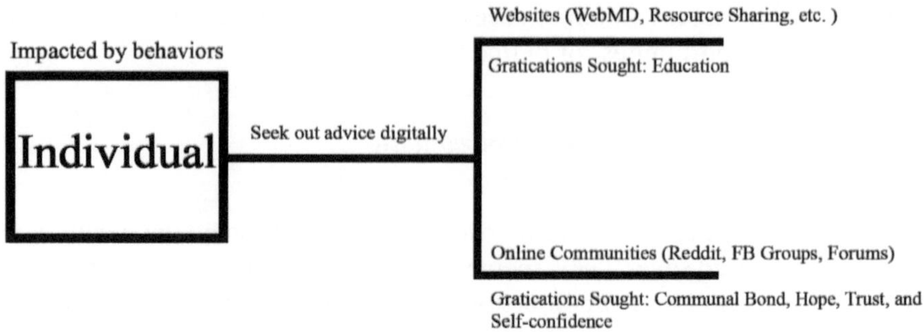

Figure 4.1 Online Gratification-Seeking Framework. *Source*: (Henderson & Pitts 2022).

trust in the community, and (3) self-confidence of the individual. In order for the user to fulfill the remaining three gratifications outside of the communal bond, it requires time and investment into the community. The achievement of hope, trust, and self-confidence does not solely rely on the user participating. The community has a substantial responsibility to facilitate an environment that provides specific goals. This becomes a challenge as online areas encompass a diverse group of participants with different beliefs and lifestyles. With the challenges of not seeing facial or body language, comments or posts may be misinterpreted. While text comments may offend users, there are often guidelines or rules that are communicated in the group. However, with a lack of group leadership through moderators or administrators, certain communities could become toxic for the users and result in an increase in behaviors, bullying, or verbal altercations. With a group that is accessible to the World Wide Web, communities become an eclectic base of personalities.

Social media provides different gratifications for each personality that uses the platforms. All platforms have audience members from different parts of the globe with different cultural and adapted norms that may be challenged in the online world. Online worlds provide different opportunities and self-seeking factors for each user, depending on their unique personality traits. For example, social networks provide users who are categorized into the self-damaging behavior of narcissism, the ability to "pursue their goals of self-enhancement, seeking attention and being admired" (Liu & Baumeister 2016, 85). Creating a network of friends on an online social platform may help lonely individuals who struggle with self-damaging behaviors, low self-esteem, and feelings of social rejection. Through this network of friends, members may become less lonely through the fulfillment of attention (Leary 1990; Liu and Baumeister 2016; Cacioppo, Fowler, and Christakis 2009). This gives users, with differentiating levels of high and low self-esteem, a place to increase connection and engagement with users with similar qualities such as sadness, stress, and anger (Aubrey and Rill 2013; Brandtzæg 2012; Valenzuela, Park, and Kee 2009; Gould et al. 2002).

Social media has provided a community for providing and receiving support. However, personalities continue to impact the determining factors of online group therapy. Certain individuals may feel safer on anonymous platforms such as Reddit compared to identifying sites like Facebook. Whichever identifying choice is made regarding social media activity, both options provide a promising impact on users, weary of the real-world conversation of behaviors. In addition, individuals with low self-esteem rely more on Facebook for personal understanding (Ferris and Hollenbaugh 2018).

Though the researchers have discussed the four main gratifications sought, there are secondary gratifications based on personality traits, as presented in several studies. Facebook also offers opportunities to connect with friends and expand friendships, which could also decrease the Facebook user's loneliness as they develop an intertwined relationship between physical and digital means (Tartaglia 2016). Facebook groups provide users with an opportunity to connect through communal bonds and provide a face and name to the connection. This creates a stronger bond with the user as identifying information is shared on account profiles (name, location, pages liked, etc.). Secondary gratifications outside of the researcher's main four gratifications vary on each platform. According to Ferris and Hollenbaugh (2018), five Facebook motives served to prove as uses for Facebook gratifications sought from the user: virtual community, companionship, exhibitionism, relationship maintenance, and passing time, which are all met in a behavioral community.

With these gratifications, the research could assume that these factors could continue to complement Levy and Windahl's 1985 concept of subconscious, preconscious, and structurally conscious impact during the involvement in the exposure stage of the concept of audience activity.

With social media use, online community groups allow users to interact more relationally with others, based on a common theme or lifestyle, in comparison to social media newsfeeds where the user is connected to everyone they are friends with. In 2015, researchers Anastasia Aldelina Lijadi and Gertina Johanna van Schalkwyk investigated Facebook focus groups with third culture kids (TCK). In their research, the authors articulated five qualities that are unique to Facebook's special interest group feature.

1) Post and share relevant information beneficial for group members
2) Raise awareness on certain issues related to the special interest group description and purpose
3) Raise questions on certain issues
4) Get consensus or gain understanding about another member's perspective on certain issues

5) To “meet” new people who share similar interests. (2–3)

In this section, the authors will share examples of how users in self-damaging behavior communities are able to meet the qualities of a special interest group defined by Lijadi and van Schalkwyk.

Lijadi and van Schalkwyk: “*1) Post and share relevant information beneficial for group members.*”

Self-Damaging Behavior Communities: Users are able to share resources that have helped them in previous events of behavioral activity. As mentioned before, users are using digital content, online support groups, and other services to seek out medical resources. While all results may provide a beneficial outcome, there is a clear opportunity for users to engage with others in online communities that prove beneficial for others. As one participant in our qualitative study stated: “*It* [Reddit] *gave me feedback on my own problems, but also by giving feedback to other people's problems, it allowed me to feel like I was doing good for the community.*”

Lijadi and van Schalkwyk: “*2) Raise awareness on certain issues related to the special interest group description and purpose.*”

Self-Damaging Behavior Communities: The group allows users to create a communal bond of awareness. The certain issues mentioned are the behavioral aspects that bring the members together. Certain issues may include advice on recovery or behavior interruptions. Groups focus on issues to fulfill the purpose of centralizing conversation about behaviors. A participant described the purpose of the group as a place of connection. When asked if community involvement increased or decreased triggers or thoughts, the participant stated, “*Better now, I want to say, because I have somewhere to go to. Whereas before, I would mostly go to my best friends, and I felt like a burden to them.*”

Lijadi and van Schalkwyk: “*3) Raise questions on certain issues.*”

Self-Damaging Behavior Communities: Users are able to generate questions that they may be fearful about or embarrassed to ask in a professional or personal setting. Anonymity is important with a large percentage of users. The questions asked could be more personal and embarrassing if shared outside of the group with identifying information. “*I share a lot more information on Reddit and especially (redacted subreddit), um, very kind of graphic descriptions of what you're feeling, what you're thinking. So I find it very, very personal.*”

Lijadi and van Schalkwyk: “*4) Get consensus or gain understanding about another member's perspective on certain issues.*”

Self-Damaging Behavior Communities: The intertwined relationship between users allows a personal and customized engagement for various perspectives to have input on questions presented. This becomes one of the core features of an online community. In one instance, a participant used communities to engage with while dealing with agoraphobia. "*I was agoraphobic. I wasn't leaving my apartment at the time. Even going down the hallway was terrifying. Just having like a source of people I could actively talk to and discuss things with was extremely helpful.*"

Lijadi and van Schalkwyk: "*5) To 'meet' new people who share similar interests.*"

Self-Damaging Behavior Communities: Users are able to generate friendships based on the behaviors that connect them. For example, one participant shared that they look for "*like-minded, people who have the same experience, people that I could talk to and share stuff with*" [in communities.]

While there are gratifications met upon joining the group, some users seek out the group due to the exhaustion of other resources. In an in-depth interview, a participant explained the difficulty of finding a group therapy for individuals with self-harm: "*I had tried other chat rooms that were signed for . . . like addiction and stuff like that. But I found that a lot of the people on those struggled with drugs and alcohol, and they couldn't relate whatsoever to self-harm. And I had tried going to a meeting, but there's no meetings for people who self-harm. So I tried in a meeting, and they couldn't understand the whole concept of self-harm. So, I had already had an account on Reddit. I did a lot of the exchanges, like the Reddit gifts and stuff like that. And so earlier with Reddit, so I just figured I'd give that a shot too.*"

As mentioned before, the responsibility for the gratifications sought does not fall on the social media platform where the community resides. Rather, the fulfillment of the gratification is dependent on the personal will of the user. The relationship of collaboration on posts has resulted from the actions of group members.

Personal Will

Creating or joining a behaviorally focused community would support the common bond that many users seek in online groups. However, it does not rely solely on the group itself. In order to meet the gratification, users have to dedicate a willingness to seek out the group and engage with posts. Even though a large percentage of the most searched pieces of information online are health articles and advice, online communities provide an engaging and personal experience that is based on online actions (Lerman et al. 2017). This supports the theory that many gratifications rely on the individuals' actions, as noted by Wenner, Palmgreen, and Rosengren (1985). With this thought, joining a group and actively engaging within the group could fulfill the gratifications of trust, hope, communal bond, and self-confidence sought from social media users. One primary issue with using an online community as a mode of therapy is that joining a group does not accomplish the full framework of communication theory. When a user joins a group, it accomplishes the transition of the receiver to medium, which only fulfills half of the theory. Without engagement in the group, the theoretical flow does not follow through to the user receiving the message (gratification). Therefore, the fulfillment of any gratifications, primary or secondary, falls primarily on the users' actions and engagement in the group itself.

Goals of Community Therapy

Individual goals may differentiate between users, but the common gratifications sought from the community and users are focused around communal bond, hope, trust, and self-confidence. With a broad perspective of the types of behaviors impacting users' lives, certain goals may have higher importance than others. Behavior modification may be important to some while providing support may be a larger concern for others in the community (Cobb, Graham, and Abrams 2010; Cobb et al. 2011). In order to move toward the goals, online communities allow users to engage with two-way communication in groups that have a roster of similarly diagnosed individuals (figure 4.2). This empowers the community participants to share in difficult conversations that may have been impossible to share in traditional therapy or in a real-world situation (Walther and Boyd 2002, as cited in Wright et al. 2003). According to Wright et al. (2003), online support communities provide users with an online location where they could find support that is not provided by healthcare practitioners or other professionals. Online communities provide opportunities for users to interact with support and discussion of behaviors while remaining in the comfort of a digital community modality (Wright 2000).

Therapies have been utilized in group settings since the findings of successful results in the early 1900s. Previous studies have used group cognitive therapy for individuals diagnosed with anxiety and mood disorders (Schachter 2011). In the work *The Theory and Practice of Group Psychotherapy* by Irvin Yalom (2008), it was found that there are eleven "therapeutic factors" to make group therapy effective.

Figure 4.2 User Community Gratification Framework. *Source*: (Henderson & Pitts 2022).

These "therapeutic factors" include:

- Universality
- Group Cohesiveness
- Altruism
- Instillation of Hope
- Imparting Information
- Development of Socializing Techniques
- Imitative Behavior
- Corrective Recapitulation of the Primary Family Group
- Catharsis
- Existential Factors

Each factor was believed to be beneficial in treatment during group therapy, as indicated in Yalom's studies (2008). In group therapy, the community has taken the main focus off the individual and has become an entity in itself, allowing the group to take on the behaviors and outcomes as a common behavior support system (Schachter 2011). This can be compared to Hillery's social interaction of "common life" type of community as the group absorbs the individual's problems as their own (1955).

An important factor that also makes group therapies very effective is the ability to show compassion and a sense of belonging. As one participant stated regarding providing support for other users, "*It* [Reddit subreddits] *gives me a sense of accomplishment and sort of like feeling good about my contributions to society.*"

The online communal discourse of emotion is a unique form of therapy. The modality of the community prioritizes emotions as the primary content for interaction. Through the online community, users can share emotional experiences to gather information about behaviors that could be considered self-damaging (Bar-Lev 2008). While members are able to share information with each other in the community, the digital relationships formed are often classified as Granovetter's 1973 "weak-tie" relationships, founded on strangers' similar behaviors (Harper 2016). However, this may prove to be beneficial for users as the weaker ties allow relationship participants to contribute toward and listen to diverse opinions based on previous experiences without the fear of a strong-tie relationship knowing the details of the conversation (Albrecht & Adelman 1987). Self-esteem, connectivity, and social support increase whether the ties are strong or weak. Thus, even the weakest of ties may improve an individual's psychosocial well-being (Buglass et al. 2017; Davis et al. 2015). In addition, the researchers believe that in order for an online community to be effective, the factors of a communal bond, hope for recovery, trust in the community, and self-confidence, along with engagement with community members are the key components of a healthy community to be effective (Liu & Guo 2015; Robinson 1988; Lijadi and van Schalkwyk 2015; Barak, Boniel-Nissim, and John Suler 2008).

Selective Coding Based on Literature

Communal Bond and Hope

After engagement occurs in online communities and the sharing of firsthand shared experiences of living with the self-damaging behaviors, users may find hope for recovery. While physicians are capable of providing valuable facts, they cannot fulfill the need for real-life experience that can be shared among online community members (Preece, 1998). Finding hope for recovery is easier online compared to real life since users can discuss with others who have similar lived experiences, resulting in a communal bond (Braithwaite, Waldron, and Finn 1999). As one participant stated: "*It's also good* [the community] *from an emotional point of view to know that there's other people in exactly the same position as you, all over the world. So it's comforting.*"

The goal of therapeutic communities is to create a bond between users to facilitate a community based on Tönnies's village (1957). The groups provide a location to discuss the communal illness, ask questions, and share concerns that may be affiliated with the illnesses (Wright 2000). When users are in the discovery process of communities that are discussing self-damaging behaviors, they are looking for other users who will listen. While health-care providers do provide a unique discussion regarding medicine and care, the care is limited due to the lack of experience with personal issues. The medical providers cannot provide the level of support that online communities facilitate due to the lack of behavioral experience (Wright et al. 2000). The community provides unique combinations of experiences, and the hope for recovery is based on the collaboration between users who have recovered, who are in the process of recovery, or who are seeking advice.

The communal bond is created between users through familiarity with a common way of life and beliefs. Sharing posts that are emotionally driven in the community will shape the emotional experiences and the life outlook of the users (Bar-Lev 2008). Behavioral experiences act as the common bond that is needed for the community. While users engage with the content, actions pursued in the groups may lead to a personal sense of control when it comes to the user's self-damaging behaviors. The collaborative nature of the community may lead to weak-tie online relationships between same-behavior users (Wright et al. 2003). Relationship bonding would provide a communal bond between like-minded users. Through the engagement of the online community, participants are able to take part in new opportunities to extend the number of their online relationships (Wright 2000).

Trust and Self-Confidence

Vulnerabilities are shared in online communities, which makes trust difficult to obtain. Giddens's form of "pure relationship" describes the action of sharing feelings with others through mutual trust and happiness (1999). Applying Giddens's "pure relationship" to the uses and gratifications theory, individuals are able to join a group with the mutual goal of gaining trust gratification found from shared experiences. This creates an intimacy between users, which sets up "the pure relationship" model of "mutual self-disclosure and appreciation of each other's unique qualities" (Jamieson 1999, 1). While users are quick to share authentic experiences, the identities of contributors are anonymous in communities such as Reddit. This could create barriers to trust in anonymous communities (Reddit, Whisper, Twitter) since users are not expected to have a verified identity, unlike Facebook.

In the majority of online communities, there are no mandated submission quotas that users have to meet. As a result, posts may be randomly submitted by various users. This creates a community that results in connecting users who have accidentally encountered posts (Bar-Lev 2008). While the posts are curated by the platform algorithm, trust is given upon exposure to the post. The users are able to share memories and experiences with the community through crafting a post that users will be able to identify and relate to with others on a personal level (Lomsky-Feder 2004).

In addition to gaining trust, users could also increase self-confidence by sharing lived experiences. Through this process of outward expression, the user taking part in communication is "essential to patient empowerment" (Barak, Boniel-Nissim, and Suler 2008, as cited in Peng et al. 2019). The personal recollections of the narratives allow the users to create their own personal versions of the stories, which could create confidence in oneself (Lomsky-Feder 2004; Kingod et al. 2017; Walsh and Al Achkar 2021). Through the sharing of stories crafted through the lens of personal emotional experience, it facilitates an empathetic community (Bar-Lev 2008).

Strand, Eng, and Gammon (2020) stated that participants found a sense of openness after sharing similar life experiences in the online community. The openness of behavior-impacting events revealed that users were not alone in their experience, resulting in self-confidence. As participants continued to share, more communities were created based on trust in each other and newly found self-confidence. According to Strand, Eng, and Gammon, reading others' stories reflected a lower sense of "shame and abnormality" (2020, 6). The authors also found two main themes: "Balancing anonymity and openness" and "enabling connectedness" (2020, 5). With the two themes presented, the participants displayed trust in the community, in addition to self-confidence in themselves in response to the openness of the community. The sharing of lived experiences proved that the users were not the only people dealing with similar thoughts or behaviors (Bar-Lev 2008).

In addition to sharing memories, communities provide an environment where users can ask questions, share thought-troubling opinions, and speak and engage in a way that would be embarrassing for their public life (Wallace 1999). Online communities do provide challenges in management and moderating. Trust and self-confidence are built through the users' interactions with the group, which could be broken if communities become toxic and harmful to the user from lack of proper moderation. Wright (2000) found that the anonymity in the community allowed the users to discuss their behaviors with other members without the underlying thought of judgment. Trust is also given to the group members as users share information that would be counterproductive or embarrassing to share with close friends or family members (Wright et al. 2003).

Through the collaborative nature of social media, continual conversations lead to a deeper knowledge of members' lives and behaviors. Developing a connection that is built on trust, the digital connection starts to behave like face-to-face relationships as users gain credibility (Wright 2000). Individuals cannot deem themselves credible to the community, but rather, they have to prove themselves through the usefulness of their contributions to the group. If a member does not gain the unmentioned status of credibility, any effort to showcase empathy or support would be difficult to communicate (Wright 2000).

There are working communities that are focused on the recovery of the users. But there are other groups where the focus is less on recovery and more on recognizing that decreased feelings toward self-damaging behaviors are a worthy goal. Upon research, groups have been found to promote behavior by decreasing (Shahab and McEwen 2009) or enabling dependent guidelines enforced by moderators. The community provides a foundation of support. With the behaviors mentioned, the users are seeking gratifications of communal bond, hope, self-confidence, and trust. As users find new ways to cope or use the community itself as a mechanism, that would provide the gratifications sought. Coping strategies promoted through engagement provide a healthy alternative to the behavior mentioned.

Chapter 5

Relevance among Online Community Users

Criticism of the uses and gratifications theory has often focused on the ability, or lack thereof, to identify the categories of uses and the categories of gratifications in measuring media content for the usage and gratifications. Scholars have suggested that the methodological approaches used to test the uses and gratification theory have fallen short because of issues related to instrument design. Dennis and DeFleur (2010) traced the development of the uses and gratifications theory and suggested that when researchers conducted studies related to the theory, often the list of each category within the studies varied widely within the scope and variables of focus. What was not disputed in the findings of the initial studies in testing uses and gratifications was that, instead of the media having a powerful effect on consumers, the data showed there were limited impacts, but more importantly, the audience was actively seeking and selecting information to attend based on individual differences, social categories, and social relationships (Dennis and DeFleur 2010; Lin 1996; Katz, Blumler, and Gurevitch 1973; McLeod and Becker 1974).

To address the criticism of past studies that focused on uses and gratification found in the study of legacy media and, more recently, in the study of mediated communication, we felt it important to use a dual methodological approach to examine online therapy communities. The ability to better understand online therapy communities and the relationship of people within the therapy communities was first examined in a pilot study conducted in 2019. Using a dual methodological approach provided us with the opportunity to discover what variables impacted online therapy community engagement. Wimmer and Dominick (2013) suggested using both qualitative and quantitative methodological approaches to understand any communication phenomena that worked best to provide insight into any variables that examine relationships between active audience members and various communication platforms and the content within the platforms. The duality of the approach was first tested in the initial phase of the study in 2019. In-depth interviews and a quantitative survey were deployed. This initial phase of research gave the authors an opportunity to test our methodological approaches and thus helped to determine the path for the larger study conducted in 2020.

The quantitative data collection instrument was designed to better understand people's motivations and usage of online therapy communities. Finding individuals who had experience with online therapy communities was a limitation of the pilot study. Initially, the hope was to have a sample size of 200 people, using a variety of tools to reach individuals who would be willing to complete the survey. Ultimately, the study reached 100 participants who were willing to participate in the study (Henderson and Pitts 2019).

INITIAL RESEARCH

The initial research for this book was guided by four areas of focus: rate of decreased harmful behaviors after engaging with online support communities; differences in content and support systems for physical versus online groups; the prevalence of social media addiction among individuals who need support group; and the motivations for seeking out online communities. The authors believed that *engagement in an online support group would decrease thoughts about harmful behaviors.* Damaging thoughts would decrease through a community environment. It would occur even more so when exercised in a group therapy environment, such as a common bond group, as Buglass et al. (2017) suggested there would be a decrease in harmful thoughts because of "social support, connectivity and self-esteem" (p. 248). Likewise, in the initial work, the authors felt they would find that *being engaged with an online support group would create higher self-esteem among users.* As Facebook increases feelings of connection in various parts of life, individuals have found that social media allows them to develop both physical and digital relationships (Ferris and Hollenbaugh 2018). Through these relationships, high self-esteem will result as they find a sense of belonging. *The sense of belonging in online groups created by common bonds, such as a common diagnosis, will create a more connected and supportive group due to common life-impacting situations.* In a study focused on youth depression within Facebook groups, it was found that Facebook groups provided a "positive, safe, and nonjudgmental environment to allow for self-disclosure and connections between like-minded youth. This aligns with other research that examines how youth connect regarding mental health difficulties online" (Lerman et al. 2017, 734). Through this common bond of a diagnosis, individuals find a community to be heard. With increased connection, *engagement in an online support group will increase emotional openness in social media users.* In other words, individuals who are seeking help regarding sadness, stress, and/or anger are researching online for various avenues of help (Lerman et al. 2017). Avenues of help from digital content, online support groups, and other services yield beneficial results where there is a clear opportunity for users to engage with others over "their experiences and potentially obtain social support" (Lerman et al. 2017, 734).

Finding people who are willing to share their experiences and engagements with research is no small undertaking. While most people deal with mental health concerns, a smaller number experience self-harming thoughts and behaviors, and an even smaller number are willing to engage with researchers who want to better understand how different modalities of mental health care are delivered. Traditional and nontraditional tools for finding a sample to participate in this work were used in the initial collection of data.

The quantitative data was gathered by creating subreddits posts focused on self-damaging behavior that provided anonymous interactions. The subreddits that were asked to be part of this study were called r/selfhelp, r/depression, r/f—eating disorders, and other similar communities (Reddit 2008d, 2009, 2014a). In requesting permission from the moderators that maintained behavior-focused subreddit communities, they were made aware of the posts, and a few were granted permission to use the subreddit communities as part of the research. These communities had an ample amount of individuals who were available to engage in the research. At the time of this research, r/selfhelp had 35,560 readers, r/depression had 467,943 readers, and r/f—eating disorders had 7,200 readers in the communities (Reddit 2008d, 2009, 2014a).

At the end of the quantitative survey, the participants were asked if they would be willing to participate in an in-depth interview. By indicating their willingness to be interviewed, each participant was rewarded with a $10 Starbucks gift card. From this group, eight willing participants were randomly selected to participate in one-on-one interviews with the researchers. The in-depth interviews provided more input and a richer data set for the researchers to use in addressing the research questions and hypotheses. This allowed the researchers to measure trends and emotions that were a direct result of their involvement in online communities.

Data was collected that would allow the researchers to assess the impact of online communities, the positive or negative outcomes participants had with online communities, an individual's social media habits toward online media communities, and the types of engagement by differentiating between physical and digital relationships where the focus was on (1) Interaction, (2) Anonymity or Identification, and (3) Differences in Physical or Digital Relationships. Moreover, the initial research sought to examine social media addiction among the participants in the study. Lastly, the initial research tools were used to determine motivations sought by using online communities.

INITIAL DISCOVERY

There were one hundred respondents who participated in the initial research. The participants were recruited from both anonymous platforms Reddit and Whisper and the identifying social media platform Facebook through the engagement of online communities. The study's subreddits were r/mentalhealth, r/anxiety, r/depression, r/stopselfharm, and r/samplesize (Reddit 2008e, 2008f, 2009, 2011, 2012). Two Facebook groups that focused on depression and anxiety were also used to recruit participants. Whisper groups on depression and self-harm were also used.

Among the 100 participants, 24 percent were male, while 69 percent were female. The remaining participants, 7 percent, considered themselves as other: nonbinary, gender-fluid, and so on. The majority of the participants, 42 percent, were between eighteen and twenty years of age. The second highest age demographic, 21 percent, was twenty-one to twenty-five years old. The next group of participants, 10 percent, had the age range of twenty-six to thirty years. Following that group, 15 percent were thirty-one to thirty-five years of age. Then, 7 percent were thirty-six to forty years of age. Two percent were forty-one to forty-five years of age. Another 2 percent were forty-six to fifty years of age, and 1 percent was fifty-one plus years of age.

For platform of choice, it was found that Facebook was selected thirty-four times (34.34 percent), and Instagram was chosen thirty-two times, 32.32 percent. This revealed that the identifying platforms were the most used out of the entire audience. Reddit was the highest anonymous platform with twenty-five users, 25.25 percent, selecting that variable. Only descriptive data was collected in the pilot study.

Fifteen Likert statements were used to determine *the rate of decreased harmful behaviors after engaging with online support communities.* The majority of the respondents, 73 percent, indicated they were more active online than in the physical world ($x^2 = 21.36$, df = 1, p = .001). And 84 percent indicated they actively sought out what people post from groups or online communities based on similar struggles ($x^2 = 46.24$, df = 1, p = .001). Sixty-three percent of participants said when they are online, they do not feel alone ($x^2 = 6.76$, df = 1, p = .01). Fifty-eight percent of participants indicated they have friends online who listen to them. Most, 72 percent, believed they have online friends ($x^2 = 19.36$, df = 1, p = .001). The majority of respondents, 82 percent, indicated they are more confident when they are online ($x^2 = 40.96$, df = 1, p = .001) and the majority, 83 percent, felt like people online understood them ($x^2 = 43.56$, df = 1, p = .001). Eighty-four percent of the respondents indicated that they believed community members inside social media groups who focused on their behaviors understood them ($x^2 = 46.24$, df = 1, p = .001).

When asked to indicate whether their recovery was made easier by an online community, respondents were divided on their level of agreement; however, there were sixty-two participants, 62.63 percent, who disagreed with the statement: "My recovery has been worse due to online communities" ($x^2 = 6.76$, df = 1, p = .01). When asked if the participants struggled with others online, forty-eight, 48 percent, of the participants agreed with the statement while forty-three, 43 percent, disagreed. And 50 percent of respondents indicated that thoughts of harmful behaviors had decreased while being a member of an online therapy group. Thus, respondents indicated that recovery was made easier by engaging with online therapy groups and 50 percent of respondents indicated that thoughts of self-damaging behaviors had decreased while being a part of online therapy groups. It is important to note that even a 1 percent decline in self-damaging thoughts is a step in the right direction.

The initial research that led to the larger focus of this book explored the type of content and support system among physical support groups and online support groups. Participants in the study indicated that they did engage with online therapy groups. Engagement could be identified by posting on the page, liking a post, or commenting on a post. Seventy-three percent of the participants said they did comment on posts inside online therapy communities ($x^2 = 21.16$, df = 1, p = .001). When addressing online communities that allowed for anonymity such as Reddit, 63 percent saw themselves as commenters ($x^2 = 6.76$, df = 1, p = .001). The majority of respondents, 85 percent, preferred to engage anonymously within online therapy groups ($x^2 = 49$, df = 1, p = .001). Privacy was a primary concern of respondents, with the majority, 90 percent, indicating the need for privacy in their online discussions ($x^2 = 64$, df = 1, p = .001). And, not surprisingly, 83 percent of respondents indicated that their closest friends are from physical friendships and not online friendships ($x^2 = 43.56$, df = 1, p = .001). However, almost 70 percent of respondents indicated they felt safer discussing online as compared to face-to-face conversations ($x^2 = 16$, df = 1, p = .001). In fact, 82 percent of respondents said they had discussed topics online that they had never talked about outside of their online discussions ($x^2 = 40.96$, df = 1, p = .001). Thus, while face-to-face friendships are important, respondents indicated they were more comfortable discussing certain topics with online friends under the anonymity umbrella within online therapy communities. It is important to note that online therapy communities can play a role in the overall well-being of participating members.

A majority of respondents, 61 percent, indicated they rarely spent time thinking about social media or planning how to use it ($x^2 = 4.84$, df = 1, $p = .05$). Thus, participants saw social media as a tool and not a necessity in their lives. Social media was used by participants, 46 percent, to escape from personal issues. Much like past forms of media that have been used to escape from the day-to-day grind of life, this does not necessarily mean the participants were escaping to online therapy groups. It simply means that they used social media for a variety of purposes that can go well beyond seeking out online therapy communities. Most do not see time spent with social media as an addiction; they simply use it for the practical purpose of escape. However, about half indicated social media use rarely has a negative impact on their job or studies.

More than 50 percent of participants (54 percent) in the research stated that they were not seeing a professional counselor, while 43 percent of participants saw a counselor one time a week. At the same time, 45 percent had thought about seeking additional help outside of their professional counselor. Participants were motivated to use online communities to help them with their self-damaging behavior journey. Forty-two percent of participants chose companionship, and 22 percent of participants who used online support groups did so to forget about the real world. Another 14 percent said they used the online support group to pass time, and 10 percent used the online support group to find happiness. Thirty percent of the participants reported that they found happiness when interacting with a professional counselor. Twenty-eight percent were motivated to seek help from a professional counselor in order to have companionship. Fourteen percent met with professional counselors out of habit, and 13 percent used counselors to pass the time. Five percent sought professional counselors to help forget about the real world, and 8 percent found help with relaxation when visiting a counselor.

Engagement with online therapy communities comes in many different forms. Two of the most common forms of engagement are creating post content and responding to other people's content. Emotions may often be strong when engaging with content and with creating content. We wanted to better understand how people felt when they chose to create content in their online therapy communities. Among content creators, a sense of calmness was felt by 30 percent of the respondents, but another 29 percent felt stress when they posted online. Sixteen percent felt confident after posting, and 10 percent felt loved after creating a post. Of those who commented on other people's posts, 42 percent felt a sense of calm, 18 percent felt confident, 19 percent were stressed, 9 percent felt loved, and 8 percent felt happy. Whether creating post content or responding with a comment, no participant felt angry.

While quantitative data provides a snapshot of the larger picture of those addressing self-harming behaviors, the use of qualitative methods is extremely beneficial in helping researchers focus on the context from which the quantitative data is derived. The initial qualitative method sought to discover common themes: (1) decrease in behaviors, (2) support group content, (3) social media addiction, and (4) motivations of engagement. Eight participants, who indicated a willingness to participate, were chosen through an online random name selector tool. These participants were then interviewed on Google Hangouts and were told that it would be recorded. They were instructed to cover up, or disable, their webcam to protect their identity. The questions were open-ended to allow the participant to expand on their own response to each statement.

The researchers wanted to better understand through conversations with participants the rate of increased or decreased behaviors. This stage focused on their initial responses to the online community and other reactions to their own engagement online. The open-ended questions focused on how they found an online community, and how they felt when interacting with the community. The interview also focused on the participant's well-being, as it asked about their individual mental health state as compared to their mental health before engaging with the online therapy community.

To better understand participants, the conversations were used to examine emotional responses to physical and online groups. This provided the opportunity for the participants to reveal what they had experienced in online and physical groups. Likewise, the focus was on what posts they had engaged with and what their last post was about. This phase gathered the common trends of emotions that were brought up by the participant through their interaction in an online community.

Social media addiction and the correlation of desire for interaction in the online group was examined to determine gratifications that the participant looked for in the group and how they sought to better understand the addictive behaviors framed over the gratifications that were sought in the study. Lastly, the conversation with the interview participants sought to discover the motivations of the participant when searching for an online community. The topics of privacy, compared to identity revealing, were explored in this phase as the participants were asked about their engagement on a given platform.

With the audience gathered, the focus was on an audience that was only gathered from online platforms; thus, those individuals involved in online therapy groups could be biased based on their current experience.

Eight participants from the 100 completed surveys administered agreed to participate in a series of open-ended questions via a 15–20-minute phone interview in exchange for a $10 Starbucks gift card. The participants were guided through twenty-one open-ended questions throughout the interview. The researchers chose not to provide demographic data regarding these participants to ensure complete anonymity.

At the beginning of the interviews, the participants were asked to describe their self-damaging behaviors to ensure the validity of their responses and their engagement with the interview. They provided several different explanations of their self-damaging behaviors, ranging from self-harm to eating disorders. Participant 1 stated, *I have [been] diagnosed [with] depression, and I have an undiagnosed trauma disorder. It doesn't really fit well into the boundaries of the DSM, but it is something like that.* Participant 2 stated, *I struggle with anxiety and depression. And then I also have an autoimmune disorder, Sjorgren's, which kind of plays into those other things. So, that's mainly what I struggle with.* Participant 3 said, *Eating disorders, anxiety and depression.* Participant 4 mentioned this:

> *So I found more meaningful connections through social media and forum communities, and as for things that I personally struggle with, I have had problems with depression on and off for the past . . . I want to say 3 or 4 years at this point, maybe 5, and sometimes that does manifest in manners of spending money when I don't need to try and get some kind of a . . . reward myself or treat myself, and it's been especially bad with bad eating habits recently, even though it was something that I used to have pretty good control over. I've gained a lot of weight because of stress eating, out of control eating, and I even experienced it where sometimes I just . . . I know exactly what I'm doing, but I continue to do the behavior anyway, and I've had feelings of, that I haven't acted up, of self-harm and destruction of other objects. So those are the things that I struggle with that might relate to your research.*

Participant 5 stated, "*I struggle with depression because one of my friends died about two years ago.*" While Participant 6 stated that her behavior was "*mainly just eating disorder.*" Participant 7 shared: "*Self-mutilation and I guess just basic anxiety disorder, PTSD, and I think that's pretty much it.*" And Participant 8 stated that they were diagnosed with depression and anxiety.

The first question asked of the participants was what groups or subreddits they engaged with regarding their behaviors. Participant 1 stated, "*Usually, I'm in a mental health Discord. That's my main one. I used to be a moderator there.*" The participant continued to explain the difference between Discord and Reddit and why they chose to engage on the platform.

Participant 1: Basically, it is a peer-support server exclusively, a peer-support server. You have to have mental illness or suspect you have mental illness to be able to join. And basically, we're trying to make it to be as very accessible as possible. It's hard because if you make it accessible to people of many different disorders, then we have to partition a lot of places and to things of various trigger warning levels and what-not.

Participant 1: A lot of times they usually get frustrated because they want to talk about this here, but they can't because we're trying to partition it, so it's very inclusive. I'd say that community has overall been very effective. I know the first and last names of a lot of my friends over there, where they live, where they go to school. It's like a lot more than just that. They have personally helped me get through some shitty times.

Moderator: Yeah, absolutely, totally understand it. Would you say you're more active on the Discord rather than the subreddit?

Participant 1: Oh, yeah, definitely. I'm much more active on the Discord. The Discord, like Reddit, it's a forum. Forums aren't very, I would say, effective with the types of conversations that need to be happening for any sort of meaningful support that isn't. Here's like a list of things, so they could want to get really in-depth when I talk to someone about their shit. Just like forums, it's just not live enough for me to get really effective, in my opinion.

While Participant 1 was active on a platform that was not initially in the survey, they still provided insightful information on the gratifications sought in using an anonymous platform such as Discord. Participant 2 was the most open individual regarding their struggle. Perhaps, their anxiety and depression were fueled by an autoimmune disease, and it was inevitable to fight as compared to the hope of getting out of a depressive state like the other participants. Participant 2 stated,

> *There's two groups on Facebook: One is a faith-based one, and then the other is . . . it's more for just anybody. It's people all over the world. And I think I use that one more. And it's called the {REDACTED}. It's a lot of people with chronic diseases. And many of them also struggle with mental conditions . . . mental health conditions as well. So, I feel like it's a larger community, and they have a lot more experiences that I can relate to than the faith-based one. But I look at both.*

It was found that the majority of the users are engaged on anonymous platforms, regarding their engagement with groups that are focused on their behaviors. The common theme that was found was the secrecy the participants wanted to keep from their family members and friends on Facebook. As Participant 7 stated:

> *My family and friends are on Facebook, so I really try hard not to engage on anything on there. In Whisper, I'm more or less in positivity groups or self-harm, depression, anxiety groups, and then just various ones of those nature.*

It did become a common theme among all of the participants to keep their struggles with anxiety, self-harm, depression, suicide, and more as secretive as possible. Secrecy could be a guaranteed gratification for several of the users in the support groups. Participant 7 went on to state during this question: "*If I'm in a self-harming mood, sometimes I Google just to see what other people are going through. I'll be honest, sometimes I look for alternative methods of hurting myself.*"

The participants were asked, in regard to their diagnosis, when they became involved with the community. There seemed to be a common thread between when the participants were initially diagnosed and when they found an online community. Participant 6 stated that they were diagnosed in 2009 with an eating disorder but found the community in 2012. While Participant 8 found the community six months after their initial individual diagnosis.

It was also found that several of the participants were already active members of the social media platforms and organically accessed the groups or communities through their normal social media browsing habits. As Participant 4 stated:

> *It was something that was really brought to me more by other people that I knew, who also experienced these things, and other people I know who also just . . . they happened to browse Reddit, and they happened to see these things linked and discussed. So, I would talk about something, and I would be told, "I saw this on this board," and I would kind of be directed there.*

The participants were followed up with a question about their initial response to the community. Overall, the value of belonging and encouragement was displayed by the majority of the participants. The ability to find other people struggling with the same behaviors was helpful to several of the participants as they browsed the communities. Participant 8 explained: "*I thought it was pretty neat to see that there are a bunch of people out there having similar thoughts as I and being able to, I guess, word it in ways that I wasn't sure I'd be able to.*"

Participant 3 went on to confirm Participant 8's initial thoughts: "*I think eating disorders are very isolating. They can also be very secretive, and there could be a lot of shame around it. Finding a community of people who feel similarly and relate was just very . . . just gave me a lot of hope at that time.*" However, on top of the benefits that have been contributed, Participant 1 also stated this, "*I was like, I felt a lot less alone because I know that there are people out there, that I know there's people out there who did it other than me.*"

Though several of the participants found a common bond with several of the groups, there were also negative communities that were deemed as unhealthy and toxic to the participant's health. Participant 1 continued to explain that, while in an intensive outpatient program, they were involved with a toxic subreddit:

> *And it was also a lot of validation in terms of people [who] would say my reasons for self-harm aren't good enough or that they would feel like there was this thing of I'm a bad cutter because they didn't cut deep enough; their cuts are superficial. It was like, yikes. And then, there was another subreddit, which was kind of linked to on that subreddit, which was, that was inhumanly, I guess. It was a terrible idea. I don't know if it's still around because Reddit recently in the past few years have gotten really adamant about trying to shut down toxic subreddits. It was literally a subreddit to showing each other pictures if there's a harm, which is that terrible idea. That shit's so triggered.*

Participant 6 also explained their experience with an unhealthy subreddit: "*Well the first one I got involved with was like a bad one, like I shouldn't have been. It was one that supports eating disorder habits. So, at that, I was like it made me a little nervous. I was like, I don't know why I keep going to this website, this is like not support I should have. So that, like I knew I shouldn't be doing that, but like I couldn't help myself.*"

Although there are multiple active toxic communities, several participants stated that the healthy communities are not as active. Participant 6 continued to state, "*Then the one on Reddit, they have more of a recovery focus. That I liked. Unfortunately, it's just a lot; it's very inactive compared to the ones that . . . it's like people currently wanting to have their eating disorder habits and continue to restrict food. So those were just unfortunately, but they get a lot more activity.*"

Participant 2 also stated that the faith-based community was less active than the secular group: "*And so having a community that kind of sees both sides of it, where it's like, 'Okay, we are struggling with this. This is what God allowed, but let's have a better perspective on it.' I really like that side of it. But also there's a lot less posting and a lot less that I've been able to relate to.*"

Since the participants were active in the online communities, it has impacted their responses in a similar manner. Regarding their emotional response to the online group, Participant 7 stated, "*Just knowing like, I know that if I'm having a really bad day or something, I can go on, and just kind of post and just say like, 'I'm struggling today, or I feel like I'm drowning today.' And something like 5, 10, 20, 30 other people can respond and be like, 'Hey, we're here for you, we feel the same.' Then private messages come in.*"

Due to the subject matter at hand, several of the participants also attended professional counseling to help with the thoughts that they were diagnosed with. Participant 1, when asked about the impact of the online community on their health state over the course of their engagement, gave credit to both their professional counselor and the online community:

> *Before, it was fucking nuts. I'm not specifically talking about the communities that's been effective, not ineffective, so primarily, the one I'm in right now, the Discord. Basically, I was super, super siloed all the time. I was in PHP at the time. I was constantly having to call my therapist at PHP all the time. I was constantly in the support rooms like, I want to fucking kill myself. I want to hang myself. This is it. I'm never getting better. Why am I just still here? I'm just delaying the inevitable. Every day is just another day full of pain before I die and kill myself anyway, so why am I waiting? That was my day, so those were my worst days. Now, I'm fairly happy. I'm in a relationship. I have taken suicide off the table completely, so it's no longer something that I seriously consider. The thought may still pop into my head, but it pops out just as quickly as it pops in, and it's not something I actively consider.*

Participant 3 stated,

> *I think what I mainly look for is kind of stories of people doing well, which can encourage me—that even if I'm not doing well, that there is hope, and there is the possibility of change, and recovery is full recovery, is possible. I definitely have benefited from other people kind of sharing how they have done well in recovery.*

It was found in the research that the majority of the participants were not in an active physical support group. However, Participant 3 shared their thoughts on why the physical support group was difficult for her life:

> *It's every experience I think I have with a physical support group [that] has been really helpful. I think the hard thing is figuring out time and work, and I have a son who's six years old, so if I need childcare, so I can get to the group—it's just . . . there are all of these things that kind of come into place that make it really hard to get there. You have to be very, at this certain time, on this certain day. That can be really difficult to have everything fall into place the right way to get there. So online communities . . . you just can be a part of it whenever it's convenient for you.*

Through the use of online communities, the functionality and flexibility of the groups were beneficial for several different participants, while the physical groups required several decisions of location, time, and who is invited. Also, the use of physical groups relies on identifying factors that are easily masked by being on an anonymous platform such as Reddit. Participant 6 explained their reservations about the physical support group and identifying information: "*I've been, I guess I'm a little hesitant just from the . . . like the stigma and the judgment, and like, I'm not, I don't know, I feel like I'm not ready [for] it. I like the anonymous part of the Internet.*" Participant 3 also shared a great point regarding physical groups compared to online groups:

Well, I haven't ever been as close with people online, for the most part, because you're not showing up each week and seeing them in person and that kind of thing. But I have made one really helpful, good connection with a friend. We've been supporting each other, for gosh, probably sixteen years now. We met on an online support group. For the most part, I feel like deeper connections are made in a physical support group. It's easier to be a part of an online support group, for me.

This supports that while online groups are helpful, it is not as emotionally bonding as a physical support group. The connection in online groups is present and allows users to gather a sense of belonging and self-confidence through discussing behaviors that the community is focused on.

The participants were asked a range of questions to measure if social media addiction had an impact on their behavior, which would suggest that they were dependent on the platforms. Interestingly, all of the participants interviewed did not show signs of social media addiction. As Participant 5 stated, "*Well I just see what's happening with my friends' lives, and see if anything might happen near me—I can go and see them.*"

Several of the participants stated that they were not active social media users until later in the afternoon after work. The participants were asked if they had a location where they were always on social media, then followed this up to ensure the accuracy of their previous statement, and the majority confirmed that they spend time in their bedroom late at night. All of the participants stated that they were not obsessive social media users, presenting a carefree attitude toward posting. Participant 6 stated, "*I don't post that much, to be honest. I don't have any, I guess . . . I don't really have any significant feelings. Like if I just go for a hike, I might post like a picture. I don't really . . . it doesn't really impact my self-esteem. I know some people get like really nervous posting. I'm not . . . I don't have that much significant feeling either way.*"

The last stage of the interview asked the participants why they would choose anonymous compared to identifying social media platforms. This stage also sought to find the types of people that the participants actively engaged with online. It was found that the participants looked for a common bond with the people they engage with or share an interest with individuals who are in a place of influence (celebrities, hockey players, etc.). When asked about the reason why they would choose an anonymous or identifying platform, Participant 4 responded with his thoughts:

But there's still a certain amount of comfort with that, where I can just be detached. I can just walk away from it at any time. I can kind of . . . admittedly, I've probably fudged things in the past to my perspective, or the way that I would want people to see them, but on something like Facebook, Facebook is almost more of an obligation. It's something of . . . I have to have this to give people something. Number one: Because that's the way that people keep in touch, and that's how I have my regular presence that if people want to find me, they can. And number two: Again, I like to keep my lives separate. And even sometimes with people that I might meet in person, like people I might meet through school, I don't want to give them a username that you can look up and find my Reddit posts.

Participant 1 affirmed other participants' thoughts as well:

It's like, sometimes I just want to talk about my suicidality without being afraid of someone or cops knocking on my door. I used to be an EMT. So I know if you get a suicidal person, you automatically go to a hospital no matter what, right? I go to the hospital—they talk to my therapist—they let me go because me and my therapist got a deal. And then I have to pay an ER bill for some stupid shit that doesn't do anything.

The data concluded that anonymity does support a more open and honest dialogue between the parties involved. However, without high-level moderation through the creator or administrators in the group, the online community could become toxic, and that causes more harm than good. It was found that the participants preferred an anonymous platform apart from Facebook that they could engage with. One participant was active in online Facebook groups; however, the groups were all private, which required the participants to be in the group to see any posts inside of it. Participant 2 explained the benefits of a private group on Facebook:

I don't think I would like it just because the thing that I love about the group is a lot of these people are going through similar things. And I don't mind sharing what I'm struggling with friends, family, even strangers that are having a hard time. Like, I don't mind doing that. But a lot of times if you post something personal, like on your personal page, there are gonna be a lot of people that . . . they may sympathize, and they may empathize, but unless they're going through it, and have some of those same things, they're not gonna understand, and they may even look down on you. Or that's how I felt, so maybe, you'd get just negative feedback, and negative . . . I don't know, that people would see you in a negative way, just because you're struggling with something. So, I like the privateness of these groups because I feel a little bit more protected in . . . that we can share what we're going through, and people understand.

In conclusion, the research found that the participants sought a community that was free from any repercussions from what they all posted. While the online community did provide a bond between the members of the group or subreddit, it gave each user a level of protection, but at the same time, a sense of belonging and joint venture when it dealt with their common struggles.

The pilot study's methodological approach and findings led the researchers to move forward with more data collection using quantitative and qualitative methods in the hope of helping to identify factors that can help those struggling with self-damaging behaviors. Most importantly, the data found in the initial stages of the research led the authors to approach the larger research project with refinements of the initial study to better address the caveats of online therapy communities. The larger research examines how online therapy communities address and protect the well-being of community members, the motivations for engaging with one community over another, how behaviors increase or decrease after interacting with behavior-focused online communities, how people engage with therapy whether online or in professional settings, people's perceptions of online therapy communities dedicated to self-damaging behaviors, and the impact of online community guidelines designed to prevent toxicity in online therapy communities. The researchers expected to find that being engaged with an online support group would decrease thoughts about harmful behaviors and would create feelings of support among the online community. Likewise, individuals participating in groups with common bonds, such as a common diagnosis, would create a more connected and supportive group due to common life-impacting situation, and lastly, engagement in an online support group will increase emotional openness in social media users.

Primary Research—The Method

A mixed methodology was employed because of the success of the initial study phase in collecting valuable data that helped to explain the impact of online therapy communities. Using lessons learned from the first phase of data collection, the researchers developed a survey instrument using some of the same variables as previously used in the first phase and adding others where needed to better address the focus of the research. The survey instrument was divided into four, (1) to (4), areas focusing on the protection of users' well-being inside the online community, motivations sought in regard to using online communities—either anonymous or identifying platforms—whether self-damaging behaviors increased or decreased after interacting with behavior-focused online therapy communities, whether participants were involved in professional therapy, online therapy communities or both, and how participants engaged with online communities. The survey included fifty-five survey items that addressed the different research focus. Likewise, interview questions were developed based on the items that were most effective in the first phase, and where limitations were found in the initial phase, additional variables were added to the conversations. The qualitative data focused on the four primary areas in the quantitative data collection instrument and was extended to two additional areas that focused on perceptions of social media users toward online therapy communities and guidelines in place in online therapy communities to prevent toxicity within the community. Of course, the interview questions are dependent on the flow of the conversation with the participants. Developing rapport with the people interviewed was important, and organic conversation topics were encouraged.

Finding individuals who identified with self-damaging behaviors was a challenge. To increase the likelihood of finding a group of individuals with self-identified, self-damaging behaviors, the researchers used a multitude of social media platforms to reach out to individuals. Moderators of behavior-focused subreddits were messaged for approval of posts in the communities. After approval in various subreddits, the survey was submitted through posting or the moderator would post on behalf of the researcher. Other social media platforms were used to gather data for the survey. The Facebook groups that focused on suicide and depression were used to post the survey. The researchers also tweeted organic tweets with the link to the survey itself. To further increase participation, the survey link was emailed to university students with the hope that some might respond. Those participants completing the survey and agreeing to do in-depth interviews self-identified as having self-damaging tendencies. The authors joined the online community platform "Whisper" and posted in groups with the name "depression," "suicide," "self-harm," and so on. The group members were instructed to message the researchers for the link. Upon messaging, the user was given the link to copy and paste into their mobile phone browser.

At the end of the survey, participants were given an option to contact the researchers to further the discussion about online communities and the community's role in the lives of the participants. Six participants met the researchers through audio-only online calls. Cameras were disabled and names were anonymous to provide privacy and facilitate openness of the participants. At the end of the interview, the interview participants were given compensation for their time.

Upon completing the interviews, the researchers transcribed them through Descript software. Transcripts were then listened to again, and corrections were made to the transcription to ensure accuracy. The answers were categorized under the research focus segment and the questions that were asked. The categorization was placed in an Excel spreadsheet. Once in Excel, the content was examined, and codes were applied to each statement. The analysis used a grounded theory approach and used open coding, intermediate coding, and theoretical coding. Open coding was accomplished through each answer to the questions. Intermediate coding occurred by gathering similarly coded statements of the previously coded data to propose overarching themes. Theoretical coding was used to code the proposed gratifications sought in the community based on previous literature.

The first code, "communal bond of a topic," was used, which is unique to the online community. In traditional therapy or medicinal practices, the lack of behavioral experience presents a gap in the connection between the practitioner and patient (Wright et al. 2000). Communal bond facilitates user collaboration between individuals who have recovered, who are in the process of recovery, or who are seeking advice. The second code included "hope for recovery." Users obtain hope based on the shared lived experiences of others; another aspect that physicians cannot fulfill (Preece and Ghozati 2001). The third code, "trust in the community," was used to explain the confidence a user had in the other users and the community itself. The trust was created through the intimacy between the users' pure relationship based on "mutual self-disclosure and appreciation of each other's unique qualities" (Jamieson 1999, 1). The fourth theoretical code used was "self-confidence." The vulnerability and sharing of lived experiences provided a new perspective for users so that they are not the only people dealing with negative thoughts or behaviors (Bar-Lev 2008).

Chapter 6

Discovery among Online Therapy Community Members

Quantitative and qualitative data collection provides a rich body of data that helps researchers better understand the why behind the numbers. In the following pages, the readers will be introduced to quantitative and qualitative data that conveys the impact of online therapy communities and the relationships that exist between those who deal with self-damaging behaviors and online therapy communities and members. The authors remind the reader that they focus on the online therapy communities with the hope that the information will provide insight into the motivations that lead a person to online therapy communities and how engagement within the communities may help the member achieve a better quality of life. The focus is on elements of the therapy community and how online access to individuals who have similar self-damaging behavior battles may be used by members to help ease some of the challenges related to harmful behavior. Throughout this chapter, the reader will be introduced to people collectively who use online therapy communities so there is a better understanding of how these individuals use the online therapy communities to help themselves and others. The reader should be reminded that the authors are mass communication experts, and the focus of the study is on how social media platforms impact the ways in which the participants address self-damaging behaviors. The findings will be used to address options to provide additional care resources for individuals who do battle with self-damaging behaviors. All data collection instruments and protocols were approved by the institutional review boards of the two authors.

PARTICIPANTS

Among the 157 who responded to the questionnaire, 123 respondents, 79.9 percent, were females; 12, 7.8 percent, were males; 13, 8.4 percent, were gender nonconforming; 4, 2.6 percent, described themselves as gender-fluid; and 2, 1.3 percent, consisting of a man wishing he was a woman and someone did not want to respond ($x^2 = 348.03$, df = 4, p = .001). Three individuals left the question blank.

A majority of the respondents, seventy-eight (51 percent), were twenty-one to twenty-nine years of age, while forty (26.1 percent) were eighteen to twenty; nineteen (12.4 percent) were thirty to thirty-nine years old; eight were forty to fifty (5.2 percent); and six (5.2 percent) were fifty to fifty-nine ($x^2 = 166.56$, df = 5, p = .001). Almost one-third of the respondents, fifty, 32.5 percent, held a four-year college degree; thirty-nine, 25.3 percent, had some college degree; twenty-five, 16.2 percent, were high school graduates; twenty-one, 13.6 percent, had a master's degree; twelve, 7.8 percent, had two-year degrees; five, 3.2 percent, had less than a high school diploma; and two, 1.3 percent, held a doctorate.

Among the respondents, the majority, 121, 78.6 percent, were not married; twenty-seven, 17.5 percent, were married; five, 3.2 percent, were divorced; and one person, 0.6 percent, was widowed.

Among the respondents to the survey, Reddit was used most by 127, 80.9 percent; Instagram followed by 115, 73.2 percent; that was followed by Facebook with 96, 61.1 percent; Twitter by 69, 43.9 percent; LinkedIn by 42, 26.8 percent; and last, TikTok by 40, 25.5 percent.

Six people agreed to participate in the interview conversation and were not known to the researchers. These participants were guided through open-ended questions that sought to answer the research foci. Participant 1 was very eager to share everything he experienced. He was a thirty-one-year-old male who experienced depression between the ages of eighteen through twenty-eight. Since his recovery from depression, he spent his free time volunteering in communities and online platforms, providing support to users engaging in behaviors. Participant 2 was a twenty-six-year-old female who worked in a mental health nonprofit. She started using online communities in 2019 when her dad passed away. Since the loss, Participant 2 sought support and an anonymous place to share thoughts of suicidal ideation. The nonprofit did not provide adequate health insurance for mental health treatment, which resulted in seeking help through online means. Participant 3 was a thirty-three-year-old female and was a moderator for a self-harm-focused group. This participant was now focused on providing guidance in the community rather than receiving any direct benefits. She had previously engaged in self-harming behaviors and discovered the group through a

Google search. Participant 4 was a thirty-one-year-old married female who was a stay-at-home mother. The participant shared that she experienced a major case of agoraphobia. With the stay-at-home status, the participant sought an activity in the community and took a moderator role. Participants 3 and 4 also had experience with toxic communities in the past and now sought to provide support to users seeking help online. Participant 5 was a twenty-seven-year-old single female who works as a Pro Re Nata (PRN) *as needed* therapist at an eating disorder treatment facility. This participant currently is involved with depression, anxiety, and anorexia. Anorexia has been active in her life for over ten years. Participant 6 was a thirty-seven-year-old male who dealt with self-harm, suicidal ideation, and PTSD. During this research, this participant was on lockdown due to COVID-19. The lack of public activity due to the lockdown created a desire to find a community elsewhere. The anxiety community provided a place of comfort and communal bond.

Though the majority of participants mentioned that remaining anonymous online was important to them, they all shared information that had deep emotional meaning. The interviews with the PRN therapist and moderators were reflective of their internal desire to support and be supported through the community, and that is precisely what the online community provides in comparison to formal therapy, which does not provide communal give-and-take of support.

Our sample reflects an overall population of individuals who have or have had experience with self-damaging behaviors. Data from the National Institute of Health (NIH) and the CDCs showed that females, more than males, struggled with self-damaging thoughts, behaviors, and suicidal ideations. A national survey administered on drug use and health and commissioned by the NIH showed in 2019 that more than nineteen million adults had experienced at least one major depressive event. That is almost 8 percent of the US adult population. The greatest number was among adult females, 9.6 percent, compared to males, 6.0 percent, and the episodes were highest among individuals aged eighteen to twenty-five, 15.2 percent (Substance Abuse and Mental Health Services Administration 2019).

Using the qualitative and quantitative data collected in this study, the researchers have synthesized the data and in the following pages seek to use this data to address the research questions. As the data is explored, the reader should be reminded that 79 percent of the survey participants and 66 percent of the interview participants were female, most were twenty-one to twenty-nine years of age; 47.4 percent had a college degree or more advanced degrees; 80 percent used Reddit; and a majority of respondents indicated that they actively used multiple social media platforms to include Instagram, Facebook, and Twitter.

FINDINGS

User Well-Being

The impact of online therapy engagements was explored in the primary data collection.

Understanding the user helps us better understand how online communities can be successfully used to address self-damaging behavior (see table 6.1). A significant number of respondents, seventy-seven, 49.4 percent, reported they were actively involved in an online community ($x^2 = 140.6$, df = 4, p = .001). Most respondents reported they did not have enemies in their online communities. Most felt supported in their online community. Fifty-six respondents, 36.1 percent, indicated they considered people in their online therapy communities to be their friends, but sixty-three-point one did not think they had friends in their online therapy community. Ninety-one-point-six percent of all respondents commented *sometimes* to *very often* in their online communities; a closer look showed that 14.8 percent very often commented and another 22.6 percent often commented.

Participants are very conscientious of the impact that online therapy communities can have on their personal well-being. People appear to be finding friends in online therapy communities and feel supported within the groups. Most participants feel heard in the community and feel safe. People indicated that they recognized the dangers of online activity and believed getting into the wrong group could be dangerous for them. Most like their communities because they have membership rules that guard against inappropriate communication, and most are in groups where there is a defined moderator to ensure the guidelines are followed.

Among those who completed the survey, most believed the moderators had the members' best interest in mind when navigating the various members' posts and comments to post. Based on survey responses, members do feel that their communities protect their well-being (Strand, Eng, and Gammon 2020). Finding a space that feels safe for members is a goal among support communities. While not connected by geography, these members find themselves in groups where they feel connected to the members of the group. This emotional connection allows them to find friends within the groups, friends who support them as they manage their self-damaging behaviors. Community members feel they are being heard within the community and that there are members to support them in the journey along with moderators who work to ensure their well-being by making sure the community follows self-defined guidelines for interacting within the online therapy group. With Geography not being a factor, the chance of making connections with people opens opportunities for

Table 6.1 Protection of Users' Well-Being by Frequency, Percentage, and Chi-Square

Likert Statements	*Strongly Disagree*	*Disagree*	*Neutral*	*Agree*	*Strongly Agree*
I am actively involved in an online community.	5/3.2%	8/5.1%	10/6.4%	77/49.4** $x^2 = 140.6$	56/35.9%
I have friends in the online community.	29/18.6%	26/16/7%	30/19.2%	34/21.8%	37/23.7%
I have enemies in the online community.	103/66%** $x^2 = 208.94$	17/10.9%	18/11.5%	10/6.4%	8/5.1%
I feel supported in the online community.	5/3.2%	5/3.2%	20/12.8%	79/50.6%** $x^2 = 129.26$	47/30.1%
I feel heard in the online community.	6/3.8%	8/5.1%	23/14.7%	74/47.4%** $x^2 = 104.57$	45/28.8%
I feel safe in the online community.	4/2.6%	15/9.6%	27/17.3%	57/36.5%** $x^2 = 69.26$	53/34%
There are guidelines in the online community to protect my well-being.	7/4.5%	15/9.6%	19/12.2%	57/36.5%	58/37.2%** $x^2 = 76.31$
There are online communities that could be dangerous to my well-being.	3/1.9%	6/3.8%	14/9.0%	33/21.2%	100/64.1%** $x^2 = 207.14$
There are moderators for the online communities I am involved in.	9/5.8%	6/3.8%	20/12.8%	48/30.8%	73/46.8%** $x^2 = 105.22$
The moderators of the online communities have my best interest in mind.	6/3.8%	8/5.1%	37/23.7%	49/31.4%	56/35.9%** $x^2 = 68.55$

N may not always equal 157. *$p < .05$, **$p < .001$.

members to find lasting connections and support as they navigate feelings of anxiety, depression, and thoughts of self-damaging behaviors.

Identifying online therapy communities as a source of support gives members a chance to interact and share life experiences that may impact self-damaging behaviors. A sense of belonging in a safe place where support is provided by community members leads us to focus on the potential motivations for seeking an online therapy community membership.

In order to fully understand gratifications sought, it is important to understand the environment focused on protecting the user experience or behaviors engaged in. With difficult topics, protection of life and harm remains important to any online activity. When asked questions about this topic, it was found that users were focused on protecting each other and building a community that promotes digital support. The statements received when asked this question segment were divided into the Excel file to go through the three-phase coding process. Phase 1 of the coding process analyzed the main topic of the statement and analyzed the statements by identifying the gratification participants sought in the community. After coding the first phase, Phase 2 provided two main themes: Community Connection (9) and User Protection (8).

Community Connection (n = 9)

Interviews were transcribed through each statement and processed through the first phase of open coding. The researchers found the following codes that were later categorized in the community connection theme. The Phase 1 codes, in addition to the number of statements displayed in the ( ), were the following: (a) Connection with Users—Bond (2), (b) Connection with Users—Felt Cared For (2), (c) Building Community (1), (d) Connection with Users—Been Helped (1), (e) Provided a Counselor Role (1), (f) Feelings of Freedom (1), or (g) Found Help or Support (1).

Users found that connecting with other individuals protected their own well-being. In one case, a user was advised, "*Somebody thought you were talking too much about yourself*" in response to a comment in a post. Several communities focused on group connections rather than individual user-to-user connections. Communities do not want commenters to focus on themselves, but rather focus on the user dealing with the behavior. By acknowledging the existence of the situation, the poster will feel as if their experience was noticed. Also, the majority of users shared that the connections helped with their well-being. "*I've had many people ask me to, you know, take care of myself; ask me how I was doing. Those kinds of things really . . . they really do help a lot.*" Acknowledgment of the reality of individuals proved to not only support but is a main gratification of online communities.

In the broad theme of community connection, researchers discovered connections found in other users/leaders led to feelings of care by the community. As one participant mentioned, they connected with other users in the community based on the communal bond of behaviors. "*I think sharing my own problems with other people can help them realize that their own problems aren't that weird.*" The confirmation that others are struggling with the same behaviors provided a view of communal bond and lack of isolation. Engaging with behaviors without a community could give a sense of isolation or feelings of shame to the individual; however, the community provides the connection of other users through the same behaviors. In addition, community connection is not limited to individual behavior connection but could be found through belonging or feelings of being cared for. "*I've been posting tons of comments in the _______ subreddit and haven't been banned; that feels good and feels cared for, because what it says to me is that not everyone dislikes those types of comments.*"

One participant focused on the individual characteristics that each individual displayed through their posting activity.

> *I think it's nice to have somebody respond to you. Because I have been doing so good the past couple of years, I haven't been leaving as many posts talking about my own problems lately. . . . And I do remember really liking what the person was saying and feeling like, Okay, this person, this person was, was really smart and a really good listener and, and, very positive and helpful and inspiring and stuff like that.*

Users become memorable in online communities. Similar to popular users on other social platforms, usernames become popular and create their own reputation. In both good and positive aspects, users may engage with posts dependent on their previous experience with the user.

The reputation of usernames impacts the engagement in the online community. In Reddit communities, users can see previous comments and posts from usernames in the account details of any user. In subreddits, moderators are visible from the home page of the subreddit community. Two participants had moderator roles for subreddits and commented on how their mod/admin position provided a counselor and support position to the community. This was a very important point for both moderators and provided a sense of pride and belonging. The community would not be active or would fall into toxicity if they were not active in their position.

However, the moderator's role does include negative aspects, as they do not feel a sense of freedom. Both admins shared feelings of frustration that they are *performing* and *onstage* when in the community. "*So, I feel like I can't necessarily share as much of the negative stuff just because I want people to feel like they can come to me when they're in crisis and not come to me when I say I'm in crisis and can't check their stuff.*" As mentioned regarding the mental health practitioners resorting to online communities due to their professional life, moderators need the same escape from their own duties. In contrast, a participant who does not hold a moderator position stated, "*I do share freely. Um, I've never had an adverse response from, from sharing freely. So I'm comfortable.*" The division of escapism between the roles of participant and moderator is evident in the ability to share.

User Protection (n = 8)

User protection, coded in Phase 2, included seven statements from Phase 1 coding. Each statement supported user protection in the community. Participants stated that the community provided protection through users performing actions to prevent any harm or negative aspects coming into the community. The Phase 1 codes, in addition to the number of statements displayed in the ( ), were the following: (a) Guidelines (3), (b) Trigger Banning (2), (c) Community Protection (1), (d) Deleted Comments (1), and (e) Troll Banning (1).

A majority of the participants shared that the actions in place by the moderators and the community members were enacted for the betterment of the community. Knowing that they were in a community that protected the users provided a sense of security and confidence. Actions by members protected the users' well-being and facilitated a safe space for communal-bond dialogue. Three statements were found to discuss the guidelines and the effectiveness of the community management. Actions such as breaking rules, posting nudity, and supporting behaviors (e.g., "go kill yourself") could result in a permanent ban from a community. "*We have the rules just to protect people in the best way that we can, the only way that we can. Rules are there to back up our reasoning for why we removed them from the subreddit, because they inevitably will break one of those rules.*" In one of the communities studied, the rules stated no encouragement or methods for suicide. Rules enforced may discourage users from following through with life-impacting and life-ending decisions based on the elimination of members who comment with persuasive dialogue.

Content removed could also include comments or posts that could create discomfort in the community. Anonymous communities like Reddit have to be proactive as a community to report harmful content. Depending on the moderation, the reputation of the community is a direct reflection of how well guidelines are enforced. One participant stated, "*I mean, they, they do a pretty good job of deleting the really awful comments.*" While communities could be structured on the guidelines, there are other communities that have more freedom. A participant shared about another subreddit through a negative, toxic perspective. "*Um, r/——, is very loose in its moderation policies. There's no kind of some, some . . . subreddits have a huge list of rules and temporary sets of rules. And we just have a very general, you can't sell, can't sell services.*" Her statements and the timidness of her sharing sounded as though she were fearful of the community for some reason.

Guidelines are not just there for content monitoring; moderators may have to apply rules to ban trolls or to trigger-sensitive content. Participants share stories of behaviors and also mention scars and triggering posts they have seen in online communities. If not moderated, communities could become a photo gallery of scars. This would become triggering for users who are trying to recover from their behaviors. In addition to photos of scars, there are other pieces of content that are not accepted. "*Um, well for eating disorders groups, it's like no numbers, no talk of behaviors, but that goes down the drain really quickly*." Rules are present to protect the users; however, with a mass group, it becomes difficult to moderate all posts and comments to ensure safety. Groups may have five hundred thousand members, but only three-to-four moderators relying on their own time and resources. Groups have also adopted a more open policy that allows censoring potentially triggering images. "*They* [the community] *to an extent, allow pictures of oldest scars. It just depends on the context, and they have to put a trigger warning on it so that before somebody clicks on it, they know that it could be triggering. We monitor what they talk about.*"

Trolls and problematic users have become a nuisance in the community. "*There are rules that are in place to protect their users there. So we have guidelines that are kind of anti-troll guidelines. We have guidelines specifically that limit what you're allowed to post, which is, I don't know, for the ——subreddit, we have one. We don't allow self-promotion posts, so things that are linking to, like, a YouTube video that someone made.*" There have also been reports of popular Facebook group admins charging for their own coaching and support. While support in the group is free, for-profit schemes are harmful to the community bond.

Users who have broken rules are banned indefinitely from the online community. A ban blocks their accounts from commenting and posting. While this is effective in protecting the community users, several communities may allow them to engage in the future after an appeal process. At times, a ban may come without knowledge of what rule was broken. Several users mentioned that they were banned from another subreddit or group without knowledge of the rule broken. After efforts of contacting moderators, they have not received correspondence. "*You know, like obviously I can't. I'm not allowed to leave new comments* [in the banned community]. *And, but, you know . . . I didn't . . . I didn't think I was doing anything wrong. You know, I'd never considered that I might get banned, for what . . . for the type of stuff that I was saying*."

However, one participant shared their experience from a moderator's point of view. In this specific community, there was an appeal process where banned users could apply. "*And there have been times when, you know, I'll just . . . I'll warn someone, and if they repeat the offense, then I'll ban them. It's very rare that anyone messages back wanting a ban appeal, and when that happens, it's honestly . . . it's kind of nice because they're usually receptive to wanting to change.*"

Behavior online can result in a community bond and can contribute to the trust of the user base. However, users and administrators are still individuals with emotions and damaging behaviors that could impact the judgment of the behavior that deserves to be banned. However, a concern many users have is the mass accumulation of reports, posts, or comments that need banning that require moderator intervention. Groups are commonly led by volunteers who have full lives. This is a different structure compared to Facebook's full-time employee and AI structure that monitors reported posts for claims of self-harm or disinformation in the common newsfeed. Oftentimes, the moderators do not have the professional training in mental health to lead in a medical professional setting, but they may have lucked out to create the community at the right time and with the most searched keywords, resulting in a large volume of user recruitment.

Thematic Coding

After the first and second phases of coding, the statements were coded in accordance with gratifications found in the literature. The main gratifications were determined in each statement to discover whether users sought communal bond, hope, self-confidence, or trust in the community. The Phase 3 codes in addition to the number of statements were the following: (a) Communal Bond (8), (b) Trust (7), (c) Hope (1), and (d) Self-Confidence (0).

Users who sought communal bonds (8) shared their behavioral experiences by connecting with other individuals. The bond shared was the struggle with similar lived experiences. The bond formed relationships, which became a prominent theme in coded statements. In the interviews, participants continued to share about the people they had met through the communities. It becomes a close-knit group where the only information users have about each other are usernames. However, to establish a bond, trust has to be given to the community. With the discussions about guidelines and banning, trust in the communities remained very important to the users. Statements that were coded as trust (7) described the guidelines enforced by the moderators. While participants shared that they could trust other users, two users felt like they had a sense of freedom in the community, which provided a sense of trust. "*I do. I do share freely. Um, I've never had an adverse response from, from sharing freely. So I'm comfortable.*"

The common rule throughout the communities was to provide a listening ear to others. Any posts or comments that encouraged behaviors or could place users in a triggering state were not welcome and could result in a ban. Posts have more freedom compared to comments. Posts are the users' personal experiences, while comments are responding to the experiences. "*I think I could share freely. I'm not, I'm not like the type of person that would want to share like objectionable material.*"

The user's experience depended on the platform used. For example, Reddit allows rules to guide how members engage with one another. The anonymous confession app, Whisper, has groups in which users can join. However, confessions in depression or suicide Whisper groups may include triggering images or words. Due to the structure of the app and groups, guidelines are not enforced. One participant shared that guidelines on Whisper were "*loosely structured.*" They also continued to share that Whisper does not provide relationships compared to other platforms. In the researchers' own experiences, recruiting on Whisper was met with inquiries for drugs and other explicit content. Another participant also stated about the sugar daddy messages she received from similar platforms.

Understanding the motivations behind the use of online communities should help with future communities and the types of outreach needed to help more people. Participants in the primary phase of research indicated that they made engagement decisions based on whether the community they engaged with was an anonymous platform or one that required self-identification. The data showed that the participants in this study valued their privacy, and anonymity was important to them.

Impact of Anonymity

Within the online communities, two variables that impact interaction lie within communities: where the member's identity is known and the therapy community where the members operate anonymously (see table 6.2). A significant number of people, sixty-five, 41.9 percent, did not know anyone in the online community where they were members ($x^2 = 56.19$, df = 4, $p < .001$). A significant number of participants, fifty-three/34 percent, agreed they do feel safe in communities where a member's identity is not protected ($x^2 = 22.65$, df = 4, $p < .001$). But a significant number of participants, seventy-four/47.4 percent, strongly agreed they feel safest in online therapy communities where participants remain anonymous ($x^2 = 127.33$, df = 4, $p < .001$). Thus, on platforms like Facebook where members are perceived as less safe than in communities where identities are unknown, such as Reddit and Subreddits, activity increases within the online therapy community when anonymity is present. And, with a majority of respondents indicating how important privacy is, online therapy communities that provide anonymity and the assurance of privacy will better serve the individual members seeking help from these communities. When compared to face-to-face discussion, the anonymity provided by community members within the online groups is

Table 6.2 Impact of Anonymity by Frequency, Percentage, and Chi-Square

Likert Statements	*Strongly Disagree*	*Disagree*	*Neutral*	*Agree*	*Strongly Agree*
I feel safe identifying online communities (Facebook groups).	20/12.8%	30/19.2%	21/13.5%	53/34%** x^2=22.65	32/20.5%
I feel safe on anonymous online communities (e.g., Reddit subreddits).	5/3.2%	5/3.2%	17/10.9%	55/35.3%	74/47.4%** x^2 = 127.33
I am more active on anonymous social media communities, such as Reddit.	16/10.3%	8/5.2%	18/11.6%	29/18.7%	84/54.2%** x^2 = 120.51
Privacy is important to me when discussing online.	–	5/3.2%	12/7.7%	35/22.6%	103/66.5%** x^2 = 154.76
I feel safe discussing face-to-face.	27/17.4%	47/30.3%** x2=30.71	13/8.4%	47/30.3%	21/13.5%
I feel safe discussing online.	3/1.9%	11/7.1%	14/9.0%	74/47.7%** x^2 = 122.77	53/34.2%
People listen to me when I post online.	5/3.2%	13/8.4%	37/23.9%	73/47.1%** x^2 = 90.84	27/17.4%
People have empathy when I post online.	5/3.2%	6/3.9%	23/14.8%	73/47.1%	48/31%
I discuss topics online that I haven't told anyone outside of online relationships.	8/5.2%	13/8.4%	14/9.0%	46/29.7%	74/47.7%** x^2 = 103.74
I know someone personally in the online community.	65/41.9%** x2=56.19	25/16.1%	10/6.5%	21/13.5%	34/21.9%
I feel my behaviors are understood by my online community.	2/1.3%	3/1.9%	14/9.0%	54/34.8%	82/52.9%** x^2 = 162.71
I have one-on-one contact with other members of the online community.	38/24.5%* x^2 = 9.81	36/23.2%	21/13.5%	38/24.5%	22/14.2%
My online community understands my behaviors.	3/1.9%	5/3.2%	16/10.3%	58/37.4%	73/47.1%** x^2=134.77

N may not always equal 157. $^*p < .05$, $^{**}p < .001$.

extremely important. Among all respondents, a significant number, eighty-four/54.2 percent, indicated that they are more active with online therapy groups when anonymity is present ($x^2 = 120.51$, df = 4, $p < .001$). Privacy ranked as one of the most important variables that impacted interactions online. A significant number of the participants, 103/66.5 percent, strongly agreed that privacy impacted the kinds of discussion they entered into within online therapy groups ($x^2 = 154.76$, df = 4, $p < .001$).

Safely being able to discuss issues in face-to-face settings was hard for this group of participants, with a significant number, forty-seven/30 percent, who said they did not feel safe discussing issues in face-to-face settings ($x^2 = 30.71$, df = 4, $p < .001$). Likewise, this was further confirmed when participants, thirty-eight/24.5 percent, indicated they did not "have one-on-one contact with other members of the online community" ($x^2 = 9.81$, df = 4, $p < .05$). But with online anonymous therapy groups, seventy-four/47.7 percent of the participants felt safe discussing issues ($x^2 = 122.77$, df = 4, $p < .001$). Seventy-three/47.1 percent of the participants felt like they were heard by group members ($x^2 = 90.84$, df = 4, $p < .001$). And the same number of the participants, seventy-three/47.1 percent, indicated that group members showed empathy toward them ($x^2 = 110.26$, df = 4, $p < .001$).

Seventy-four /47.7 percent of the participants strongly agreed that they had discussed topics in the online community that they had not discussed elsewhere ($x^2 = 103.74$, df = 4, $p < .001$). And, as we would hope, the majority of the respondents, eighty-two/52.9 percent, felt like people in their online therapy community understood their behaviors ($x^2 = 162.71$, df = 4, p. $< .001$). This was further confirmed by an additional measure used to ensure construct validity of the scale, where a significant number of the respondents, seventy-three/47.1 percent, indicated strong agreement for the statement: "My online community understands my behaviors" ($x^2 = 134.77$, df = 4, p. $< .001$).

Identity protection was a common theme in the interviews. Participants shared that they decided on the platform of engagement based on the protection of identifying information, protection of self, or solely on anonymity. Protection of self included not revealing behaviors to loved ones or friends. This theme was created out of statements of possible embarrassment or fear of revealing the behaviors. The following codes were found: Protection of Identity (4), Anonymous (3), and Protection of Self (2)

Identification became a major concern in regard to platform decisions. Concerns about future jobs and social media investigators were shared. "*If you get a job, they have teams of people that scroll through social media. Um, especially if you get a government job, it's better to have your anonymity.*" The theme of anonymity was present throughout the interview, as participants were careful not to reveal information that could be traced back to who they were.

The majority of concerns dealt with identifying names being affiliated with the behaviors or discussions on the platform. The potential of connecting identities and posts created an emotional response of fear in several of the participants. One participant accidentally shared where they worked and immediately became nervous about revealing the information. "*Whereas I might, I would feel much more comfortable posting it on Reddit because I would feel like it's much less likely to be tracked down to me and attributed.*" Potential impacts of the future were evident. Participants have heard stories of how social media has caused a loss of jobs and families have found personal accounts. "I *don't think anyone really wants everything they say on a platform following them around for, for the rest of their life.*" The anonymous account became a safe space for their behavior-focused lives. "*I think I still feel to some extent that I can't really put my actual name on the internet, just because I . . . that's just . . . that's not how I started, so I don't want to do that still.*"

Several of the interview participants revealed that they worked in mental health careers but found online therapy communities were helpful in addressing their own personal mental health. Some participants revealed that while they are mental health workers, they did not feel like they had a safe place to share their own struggles even though they worked in professional mental health roles. After working in a role that dealt with eating disorders or depression, full-time professionals turned to online communities to seek therapy of their own. They provide therapy but did not feel welcome in therapy themselves due to the profession. "*I work PRN—so as needed—at an eating disorder treatment center, um, as a therapist, which really sounds super critical, um, considering given my background. Um . . . so, I just worry about the repercussions of having that sort of get out. Um . . . so, I'm very quiet about when I post it. If I do post.*"

The anonymous communities provide a safe place for unedited and more graphic content that could be flagged on other platforms. Open content policies allow people to share everything they are feeling without the fear of repercussions. "*I share, share a lot more information on Reddit and especially PTSD, um . . . very kind of graphic descriptions of what you're feeling, what you're thinking. So I find it very, very personal.*" With the promise of anonymity, true feelings are shared with the fear of repercussions.

Fear of being found out by family was also mentioned. Participants never shared that their families knew about the behaviors they engaged with. While fear was a primary motivator, it had an underlying gratification of protecting oneself. One participant shared that many families are clueless about what struggles exist among family members. "*A lot of people are comfortable being open and honest with. There's a lot of backlash, or at times, people's families won't know that this is something they're struggling with or that something happened.*" In some cases, the spouses did not know about the behaviors users engaged in. The community was a secret that users engaged in during private times.

But as time allows users to heal from behaviors, a member may be proud of the recovery progress they have made. Online communities have provided temporary or permanent homes for various stages of the behaviors. Longevity in the community depends on the goal of the user. If the goal is recovery, they could eventually be proud of the progress made and become capable of sharing past struggles with their family. "*At that time I was probably pretty depressed, or even five years ago when I lost my job, I was very depressed. So, I would not want friends or family seeing that side of me. But I don't . . . I wouldn't mind if friends and family saw what I was posting today because my posts today are much more positive and like, not so scary you know. Like, it's like . . . you know.*"

While anonymity is important in deciding to engage with the online community, there are other factors that motivate people to engage with online therapy communities or to engage with professional counselors beyond anonymity (see table 6.3). When in search of online therapy communities, participants indicated that they sought out support communities to find companionship in the group, to help them feel better, pass the time, forget about the world, relax, find more happiness or confidence, and sometimes it was just out of habit. Likewise, when seeking help from a professional therapist, participants indicated they sought out a therapist because they would help them feel better, have more confidence, be happier, find companionship, help them relax, or forget about the real world, to just pass the time, or to just do it out of habit (see table 6.3). Whether a support community or a professional therapist, participants used both to help them with their everyday living.

Table 6.3 Motivations for Spending Time with Support Groups and Professional Therapists by Rank, Frequency, and Percentage

Rank	*Support Communities*	*Rank*	*Professional Therapist*
1. Companionship	94/59.9%	1. Therapist helps me feel better	98/62.4%
2. Group helps me feel better	90/57.3%	2. Confidence	58/36.9%
3. Habit	75/47.8%	3. Happiness	57/36.3%
4. To pass the time	71/45.2%	4. Habit	37/23.6%
5. Forgetting about real world	59/37.6%	5. Relaxation	32/20.4%
6. Happiness	53/33.8%	6. Companionship	31/19.7%
7. Confidence	41/26.1%	7. Forgetting about real world	25/15.9%
8. Relaxation	32/20.4%	8. To pass the time	8/5.1%

Gratifications and Motivations

Gratifications sought to serve as the primary reasons why users continue to engage in the community. The gratifications met in the community continued to draw participants into the habit of engagement. A variety of different statements were provided in this set of interview questions. Users found gratifications that were platform specific and regarded as privacy. Coding all statements in Phase 1 was gathered into Phase 2 coding. The following codes were determined for Phase 2: Community Belonging (21), Behavior Focused (13), and Group Leading (10).

Community Belonging (n = 21)

Users discussed the ability to feel connected and to have a sense of belonging in the community. This code incorporated all the statements that referenced an intrinsic gratification of engagement in the community. The researchers found the following codes in the statements: Connection (4), Nonjudgment (4), Engagement (3), Support (2), Diversity (2), Agreement with Moderators (1), Security (1), Temporary Connections (1), Empathy (1), Positive Feedback (1), and Knowledge (1).

Personal connections proved to be a main source of gratification regarding engagement. Participants continued to share stories of whom they met online from providing or receiving support. Not only do users seek connections with each other, but users desire connections with moderators. However, moderator relationships were also viewed with bitterness due to guideline enforcement or community bans. One participant shared that they were banned from another subreddit due to posting content the moderator disagreed with. In the conversation, the participant was very frustrated that they still did not know why they were banned from the community. They eventually found a replacement for the desired community. The participant stated, "*Instead I found this other one, and I found the moderators to be much better and more suited to the topic that they were monitoring.*"

Personal connections over behaviors were desired by participants; however, they did not have a community to engage with in the physical world. They often found themselves in positions where they desired to talk about behaviors but did not want to share with friends or family. Online communities provided them a place where they could interact with others who shared the same behaviors under the blanket of anonymity. Several participants had a difficult time discovering the correct communities, as several forums or chat rooms dedicated to addiction or damaging behaviors had a direct focus on substance abuse. "*I had tried other chat rooms that were signed for, like, addiction and stuff like that. But I found that a lot of the people on those struggled with drugs and alcohol, and they couldn't relate whatsoever to self-harm.*"

The participants shared their experiences of hiding their behaviors and how isolating it felt in their personal lives. "*I mean, eating disorders are incredibly isolating.*" Participants shared how they could not reveal thoughts to family or friends out of fear of being judged. Several mentioned that their friends would not understand the behaviors at the necessary depth. However, the online communities provided a safe space for understanding. "*I was just grateful that there was a place that I could go, that with like-minded people, people who can understand it; that's really about it. And, you know . . . not be looked at like on a third head or something.*"

Connecting with the community includes diverse gratifications due to the diverse community members present. In addition to the agreement with moderators or users, the freedom to share the lived experiences with the community was very helpful for users attempting to find support. "*But you know, typing it out, people are there to tell you, you're not alone in what you're experiencing, that they've experienced it as well.*"

The communities have a diverse group of admins and users ranging in backgrounds and behaviors. Participants shared the structure with a negative sentiment. The belief that moderators had a bias or practiced favoritism within the community was evident in the interviews. While the groups acted as public forums for user collaboration, medical professionals were rarely active as moderators or users. Though there is no professional training for moderators, users still found a place of acceptance and nonjudgment. "*They're not, they're not judgmental. So I find it very positive. Overall.*" Users finally found a place where people understood their behaviors. "*People listen. I've never had anyone, anyone troll me, or put me down, um. . . . No one's ever threatened to ban me from those communities.*" The community also acted as a confession community for thoughts and actions they would never share with their physical connections. "*I liked how I could just put things out there. So, I guess, in a way, felt welcomed.*" Fear of the unknown reaction kept the behaviors from being shared with family and friends. "*I don't want my family and friends to know how deep the struggle is, so. . . . Whereas, you know, on this one app, I can just put it all out there and at least get off my chest and not have to deal with it at that moment.*"

The fear of judgment was eliminated after sharing thoughts through the community. At times, comments or posts with other users transitioned into further engagements through direct messaging or calls. "*I spent like the first forty-five minutes or thirty minutes chatting with him (another user), not giving him advice, just for listening and empathizing.*" Users providing additional encouragement were found to be very helpful and a reason for continual engagement. "*I'm mostly on there for just support but also as a way to vent because I do* [have] *very often moments of strong suicidal ideation and stuff.*"

Participants shared the positive reinforcement, knowing that other community users are listening to their posts. "*And also, just, you know, just being supportive. Yeah, when, when somebody spends time talking, chatting with you on ______, or somebody writes a lengthy response to your lengthy post, you feel like someone is listening, and maybe just then, in itself, can help you feel a little bit more hopeful.*" This promotes a safe and welcoming environment among the users. While the majority of the participants have mentioned the emotional safety of the space, one participant shared that her engaged communities were absent of drama. The absence of drama was a deciding factor in their search for a community.

Several participants mentioned the gratifications they sought from the other engaged participants. The presence of diversity, positive feedback, and access to knowledge were all deciding factors for participants. As one participant stated, "*Um, if you join a group, that's full of very similar people, um . . . in their way of thinking, then, the results that you can get from that group are quite limited.*" The participants shared how the diverse ranges of experiences, ages, and backgrounds all impacted how they perceive the group interaction. The group interaction could provide positive feedback for the participants if the community was moderated well. The community provided a collaborative environment where users could engage with each other. As the positive collaboration increased, the users' involvement could increase as well.

> *So one reason why it's so enjoyable to post on _____, it is that when you leave a comment, people will frequently, not always but some of the times, they'll reply with, "Thanks, that's helpful." And so, you know, if you leave . . . if I . . . if I leave five comments and two people reply, "Oh, thanks that was super helpful," then that's very motivating to keep participating in that community. If I had left five comments, and five people responded like, "No, you're wrong," then, that would not be very motivating.*

This engagement provides opportunities for the users to share lived experiences and knowledge. With a diverse audience, the knowledge includes a range of backgrounds and experiences. "*I really enjoy using the _______ community because there's a lot of people involved in that, and there's some very knowledgeable people in there.*" As mentioned before, gratification fulfillment is the user's responsibility. The social media platforms facilitate the opportunity for the users to engage through hosting the community. However, engagement does differ depending on the user's comfortability. All participants who were interviewed shared that they engaged with others; one participant stated, "*Almost every single post that comes on to self-harm, I comment on,*" and another commented, "*So I'm pretty much a poster and a commenter. I don't really lurk.*"

Overall, belonging is the highest gratification sought in the community. Online platforms provide users with a place where they feel comfortable sharing struggles and connecting with others. Communities also provided a listening ear when users felt like they could not share outside of the online anonymous groups. "*Sometimes it could be really good just talking to someone 'cause my best friends do know my struggle, and I just don't like burdening them with it all the time. I don't want it to be the only thing we talk about, so.*" In a technology-driven culture, online communities have provided an easier way for people to be honest with the behaviors they experience. Users do not have to hide behind secrets in their lives, but rather they can use a community to assist with recovery or confession.

Behavior Focused (n = 13)

Behavior-focused statements were found to deal with anything regarding self-damaging behaviors. Participants shared statements that focused on their behavior rather than connection. The researchers found the following codes in the statements: Behavior Modification (4), Behavior Interruption (4), Same Behaviors (3), Resources (1), and Recovery (1).

Several users used the community as a way to modify the behaviors in their lives through the connections made online. Users saw others in the community as inspirational models for their own behavior modification. Participants shared that the engagement with each other in the behavior topics felt like they belonged and were cared for. "*Finding connection in other people who are struggling with the same thing as me, like, makes me not want to engage in that behavior because I'm like, 'Oh, well, these people are doing it well.' So, I could do it well, too. And by that, I mean not engaging in behavior.*" Engagement created a healthy trajectory for users, as they were provided a model that users may emulate.

Users may have found benefits and recovery, but there were those rare toxic users at times. The toxic users had negative attitudes that demeaned the sentiment of recovery and like-minded users in the community. "*I think they're doing all right so far, the mental health communities. I mean everyone that seems to work for them, especially the big ones. Their, their motives are pretty clear—they just want to help people.*" Users did not look at behavior modification as an immediate solution but discussed it as a gradual process toward healing. The gradual process is the emulation users may act toward as a result of their engagement. Participants emphasized the longevity of the behaviors and understood recovery was not an overnight process. The community provided that common understanding and could encourage other users when they had a bad day. "*If somebody goes six months without harming, and then they have a relapse . . . they still had 180 days of good—like, you just had a bad day. That doesn't mean you have to continue down this road. Like . . . you've got it! Especially with the whole pandemic.*"

While behavior modification is a process, several users found the communities as a way to interrupt behaviors as they were happening. "*Sometimes when you're kind of having a panic attack, you've got tunnel vision, and it's good to have someone else to just lift you out of it.*" Users utilized the community as a confession outlet as they were experiencing the behaviors in real life. "*You just kind of put up what you're feeling in the moment, or, I guess, in a way, the most toxic thoughts. You know . . . like the suicidal ideation, and it's just a way to get it out there and accept it. I guess for me, it's a way to just put it out there and accept it for what it is rather than, I guess, hiding from it.*" Users may write suicide letters or confessions of self-harm with descriptive text, which turns into support in healthy communities.

Users did mention that the behavior interruption depended on the community. Certain communities were focused on behavior modification/interruption, while others may have only discussed the behaviors. "*And then where you have _______, the goal is to stop self-harm. And there's also a subreddit of self-harm where it's not to stop it. It's just talking about it. So it's where people are actively engaging in it. And sometimes they'll talk about things that are triggering or negative, and they can post pictures of stuff that they've done. So it definitely varies depending on which subreddit.*"

With a variety of communities available, curiosity was often the driving factor in how communities were discovered. One user found the community to "*just see if people are struggling with the same things.*" Bonding over behaviors allowed users to find peace and affirmation within their own lived experiences. A participant shared that they found "*like-minded, people who have the same experience . . . people that I could talk to and share . . . stuff. For a while, I followed a Reddit called Raised by Narcissists, and for a while, it was able to help deal with the relationship that I had with my mom and just realizing that it wasn't normal behavior.*"

Participants were not trying to find the community for support. They sought to understand if they were alone in their behavioral struggles. The impact of loneliness and acceptance of oneself became so overwhelming that curiosity sparked the search. Upon discovery, communities provided lived experiences, connections, resources, and recovery opportunities. Posts and comments ranged in variety. For example, one user shared their experience with posting a new resource that helped with their behaviors. "*I bought, um, an anxiety diary, uh . . . a workbook diary. Uh, somebody else recommended it. So I bought it, and I looked at it, and put a post about that.*" This post was the most recent discussion the participant shared on Reddit. It was focused on helping others with their own behaviors.

While users may have different goals in the community, participants gave partial credit to the communities for their own recovery. "*I'm doing a lot better now, but several years ago I was in a much poorer place. And I . . . you know, I, I needed heavier medication and more therapy, and now it's, it's a lot easier. And, I think, I think in part because of the communities on Reddit, it helped a lot.*"

Group Leading (n = 10)

While users connected through community belonging or behavior-focused gratifications, the researchers found that taking on a leadership role was important for several users. The moderator or admin role allowed users to provide help or support for community members dealing with behaviors. Statements were coded if participants focused on taking on a leadership role in the community. The researchers found the following codes in the statements: Providing Help (5), Support (3), Relation (1), and Out of Boredom (1).

The participants mentioned they sought gratifications of group leading as they took on a leadership role through official means (admin), or they contributed to leading the group toward healing or communal discourse. For example, one participant shared, "*I think it's really nice, especially when you know that you can actually give someone really good advice. I think it can be hard when you really want to assist someone, but you don't know how to go about it, or they're really . . . you know, there's . . . you don't have the answers that they're looking for.*"

The physical absence may provide difficulties due to the lack of body language and other factors mentioned earlier in this book. However, online communities provide an archived organization of posts with usernames for immediate connection. Archival footage is not available in physical connections, except through personal memory. Users can use previous messages in reference to current interactions: "*I actually get random messages throughout the year where somebody will message me saying that I helped them during a certain time. And they were grateful, and they came back to tell me that what I said mattered or meant something to them. So that, that, really makes me feel like I'm actually making a difference, and that's what I'm doing. But I like reaching these people and that my time and effort is not wasted.*" The ability to create an online persona and allow previous posts to serve as their reputation was valuable.

While posts may generate a large amount of engagement, there are posts that do not receive any comments. To mitigate the risks of no engagement, group leaders have emerged in the community to provide the engagement desired for the users posting. This is an important role, especially with the desired behaviors and connections that surround these communities.

> *I try to comment on the Reddit posts that have zero comments, because when you go, when you go to the subreddit, it'll show a list of posts, and some of them will have like ten comments after twenty-four hours. And someone will have zero comments after like two days. And those are the ones that I try to reply to first. So some people don't feel like they aren't being, you know, the cause of it. It's pretty depressing to post about your problems, you know, open up about your problems on the subreddit, and not hear anything back.*

The majority of the statements about group leading were actively commenting on users' posts and providing a leader's voice. Other participants shared that they provided a listening, supporting voice rather than engaging through advice or lived experiences. "*Every once in a while, I'll still join _____ as what they call a member, which is their version of venter or talker . . . but most, most of the time, listening to other people and replying to their problems.*" The community provides an ability to find what users are seeking through the leadership of group leaders.

Thematic Coding

In accordance with the literature, the codes were thematically coded in Phase 3. Statements were coded as a main gratification sought in the involvement of the community. The following codes were found: Communal Bond (24), Hope (12), Trust (12), and Self-Confidence (9).

As the researchers have mentioned, a like-minded community (communal bond) provided huge benefits to the individuals involved in the online platforms. One participant shared that they finally had someone to talk to after a crippling moment of agoraphobia. "*It* [the community] *was just super helpful. It was like a breath of fresh air. I was completely overwhelmed by everything. Like I said, I was agoraphobic. I wasn't leaving my apartment at the time. Even going down the hallway was terrifying. Just having, like a source of people, I could actively talk to and discuss things with was extremely helpful.*"

Involvement in the community often provided hope for finding assistance. "*Um, I was just kind of reading through and getting used to the community, and then one day, I really needed some help. So, I just posted on there and went into the chat.*" Finding hope does require a level of trust in the community. The validity of the communities or a mass of collective users discussing the topic often provided a sense of trust. "*I think the PTSD one I really enjoy using because there's a lot of people involved in that, and there's some very knowledgeable people in there.*" Communal bond was the most important factor in community seeking. Users have to bond over behaviors and find people struggling with the same issues. As mentioned before, users did not seek help with behaviors, they sought to understand if they were alone in their struggles.

The researchers asked when the participants first found a community. All but one of the participants shared a moment in their lives that sparked a cycle of depression or destructive thoughts about themselves. Events of fathers passing away or country lockdowns during the pandemic were all critical moments in finding a community that users could trust. The ability to discuss current event feelings with someone in the guise of anonymity created a bond between the seeking user and the community members.

Self-Damaging Behaviors

Exploring how online communities impact self-damaging behavior was the central focus of the primary research. There are many variables that may impact self-damaging behaviors. Feelings of safety when interacting with an online community were critical to the overall success of online therapy communities (see table 6.4). Ninety-two-point-eight percent of all the participants indicated they felt safe when interacting with their online therapy group ($x^2 = 193.77$, df = 2, $p < .01$). Sixty-seven, 43.2 percent, of the participants felt that belonging to an online therapy community was something that could help reduce the stresses of life ($x^2 = 127.42$, df = 4, $p < .001$). Likewise, the majority of the respondents, eighty-two/52.9 percent, agreed that the online therapy community helped them feel better about themselves ($x^2 = 76.39$, df = 4, $p < .001$), and that sixty-four, 41.3 percent, would seek support from their online community ($x^2 = 94.71$, df = 4, $p < .001$). Sixty-two participants, 40 percent, indicated that when they felt lonely, they would seek out their online community members for support ($x^2 = 61.67$, df = 4, $p < .001$). Sixty-nine participants, 44.5 percent, did believe that online communities helped them to work through issues in their chaotic lives ($x^2 = 77.3$, df = 4, $p < .001$).

Being a member of an online therapy community did help members when facing loneliness and low self-esteem. Members found safety within the community and sought the community out when the pressures of life fell onto them (see table 6.4). While still a member of online therapy communities, eighty-nine participants, 57.4 percent, indicated that they still were impacted by self-damaging behaviors ($x^2 = 159.27$, df = 4, $p < .001$). Forty-five participants, 29 percent, reported they did not simply use the online community when self-damaging behaviors were triggered but instead used the community consistently ($x^2 = 20.71$, df = 4, $p < .001$). Most of the participants, sixty-two/40.3 percent, shared that they believed their recovery had been made easier with the help of the online therapy community ($x^2 = 59.38$, df = 4, $p < .001$). Forty respondents, 25.8 percent, did not believe their recovery was made worse by their membership in the online therapy community (x^2 = 19.81, df = 4, $p < .001$). However, through self-reports, 29 percent of respondents believed self-harming thoughts had decreased while participating in online therapy communities, and 42.5 percent of participants disagreed with the statement that harmful behavior had increased.

The authors suggest that online therapy communities may be useful to individuals dealing with self-harming behaviors. The therapy communities supplied members with a sense of belonging, and that is important to the overall well-being of an individual. The impact of membership on behaviors may be affected by the length of time within a therapy community, which is something we did not test for in this study. We find that the therapy communities are helping members, and while not significant, there are members of the communities that believed the group helped them with self-damaging behaviors.

Engagement

To further understand the impact of online therapy communities on individuals with self-damaging tendencies, the in-depth interviews led us to a deeper understanding of how engagement with the communities may help an individual. To establish if communities were assisting in increasing or decreasing damaging activities or thoughts, participants were asked a series of questions about the community's impact on their behaviors. Statements were coded based on what they sought in the community. Participants may seek different gratifications based on the stage of recovery or influence of the behavior in everyday life. After coding all statements in Phase 1, common codes were gathered in three codes in Phase 2: Seeking Support (16), Intrinsic Gratifications (10), and Behavior Focused (6).

Support (n = 16)

Statements were found in this code based on the receiving or providing support within the community. The community was found to be a mutual collaboration of users giving and receiving the support and the engagement they needed in accordance with their posts. The following Phase 1 codes were found: Providing Support (9), Engagement (4), Receiving Support (2), and Confidence (1).

Support was the highest gratification found in the statements provided in the in-depth interviews. However, the majority of the support statements dealt with the participants providing rather than receiving support. Providing this support in the community produced the gratification of helping others to get through a behavior they had experienced as well. There was also a personal connection to the impact of the behaviors and the opportunity to assist with

Table 6.4 R3: Have Self-Damaging Behaviors Increased or Decreased after Interacting with Behavior-Focused Online Communities?

Likert Statements	*Strongly Disagree*	*Disagree,*	*Neutral*	*Agree*	*Strongly Agree*
I feel safe when interacting with my online community.	1/0.6%	6/3.9%	15/9.7%	82/52.9%** $x^2 = 154.26$	51/32.9%
The online community helps me cope with the stress of life.	4/2.6%	5/3.2%	16/10.3%	63/40.6%	67/43.2%** $x^2 = 127.42$
My online community helps me feel better about myself.	1/0.6%	6/3.9%	15/9.7%	82/52.9%** $x^2 = 76.39$	51/32.9%
I seek support from my online community.	4/2.6%	13/8.4%	18/11.6%	64/41.3%** $x^2=94.71$	56/36.1%
When I feel alone, I seek out my online support group.	12/7.7%	17/11.0%	18/11.6%	62/40.0%** $x^2 = 61.67$	46/29.7%
My online support group helps me work through my chaotic life.	7/4.5%	12/7.7%	32/20.6%	69/44.5%** $x^2 = 77.36$	35/22.6%
I am still impacted by self-damaging behaviors.	3/1.9%	11/7.1%	13/8.4%	39/25.2%	89/57.4%** $x^2 = 159.27$
I only engage with online communities when my self-damaging behavior is triggered.	40/25.8%	45/29%** $x^2 = 20.71$	21/13.5%	34/21.9%	15/9.7%
My recovery has been easier thanks to online communities.	18/11.7%	8/5.2%	42/27.3%	62/40.3** $x^2 = 59.38$	24/15.6%
My recovery has been worse due to online communities.	40/25.8%** $x^2 = 19.81$	37/23.9%	40/25.8%	27/17.4%	11/7.1%
My thoughts of harmful behaviors have decreased since being in the group.	17/11.0%	29/18.7%	64/41.3%** $x^2 = 54.77$	34/21.9%	11/7.1%
My thoughts of harmful behavior have increased since being in the group.	34/21.9%	32/20.6%	61/39.4%** $x^2 = 50.32$	20/12.9%	8/5.2%

N may not always equal 157. *$p < .05$, **$p < .001$.

recovery or support. As a receiver of the support, a participant stated, "*If you're kind of in a funk or having a bad day, it helps to see the positive messages that people have sent. And to know that, that, I have a purpose and a worth, to read other people's uplifting things like, 'Oh, I made it six months today,' or 'I made it one week,' just to see how proud they are.*" The impact of one's value on a community can be measured through the ratio of karma in Reddit. The more karma one has on the platform, the more their comments or posts are upvoted. The number of upvotes and downvotes create the final karma score, or as some users call it, the ratio. "*As long as most people seem to really appreciate and be sort of grateful for your comments, then you feel like, 'Oh yeah, I am, I am doing good for the community,' because my ratio of people that really liked what I said and thanked me for what I said is really good, too. Compare it to . . . you know, my ratio between positive and negative.*" The sense of accomplishment and "*doing good for the community*" provided an inspirational moment for the support providers. In a lifestyle that may be limited due to behavior limitations, they felt a sense of freedom and purpose through providing support through engagement.

Though providing collaborative support is important to the community's well-being, the responsibility of changing behaviors or mindset remains with the user engaged. This could become disheartening for users trying to provide support to other members' needs. In turn, other members' perspective of non-receptiveness impacts the providers' sense of belonging.

> It's hard when you really want to help somebody out, and they're unreceptive to it, or they'll say, "Well, I did that, and it didn't do anything for me." I think it's hurt me in a way that it's just disheartening. I don't think it's really been a detriment to my mental health, but it does kind of increase this level of pessimism as in, "Well, what am I even doing here? Is this really helping anything?"

The sense of purpose is impacted by the receptiveness of the message receiver. Support is not always received due to external factors. It is not the provider's responsibility to change behaviors—it remains the original poster's responsibility.

There are benefits to contributing support to the community. The karma-focused mindset allows users the ability to give their support, and in return, it could improve their own mental health. "*If I'm just having a bad day, I know I can go in there, and I can affect somebody else and make them have a better day than what they're having to kind of lift them up. And so doing, I lift myself up*" As users engage with others, a sense of contributing to society is accomplished. "*It gives me a sense of accomplishment and, sort of, like feeling good about my contributions to society.*" Another participant shared, "*By giving feedback to other people's problems, it allowed me to feel like I was doing good for the community.*" Users mentioned that their engagement was something they looked forward to, "*It's definitely a really fun thing to do after work.*" Users received positive responses to previous posts, which contributed to a sense of positive anticipation. "*Whereas if I've received a positive, supportive response, I guess, I would look forward to it.*" Contributions to the online therapy communities provide one of the simplest of gratifications, that of helping others, as one participant summed it up: "*It's nice being able to just help people.*"

As a support receiver, the interaction with supportive engagement decreased users' damaging behaviors. "*It really helped the social anxiety a lot, just because I've actively been having to deal with so many more people than I would've chosen to before. And, yeah, I think it has improved overall.*" In comparison to providing support, only two statements were coded as the main gratification in receiving support from the community. "*People* [in the group], *technically, if they're serious about being in the group, they give me feedback and support.*"

The communities provided an outlet for users who do not have another option of therapy. As mentioned before, participants had limitations on why they could not seek out professional therapy. Lack of health insurance and fear of leaving home were barriers to seeking help. However, the online community provided an area of support, eliminating those barriers to engagement. "*Being there on nights where you have nobody else you can talk to, or everybody else is asleep, and you just need to know that somebody cares and sees you.*" The support found in the communities creates a sense of confidence for users. "*Having this kind of little community in your pocket, you can take around with you just gives me that little bit of reassurance and bolsters my confidence.*" Users could safely share their secrets and behaviors without feelings of judgment. All participants stated that they felt safer within anonymous platforms, which mitigates the risks of behaviors being revealed to their own personal connections.

Intrinsic Gratification (n = 10)

Though support is important for group well-being, participants also focused on the intrinsic gratifications of why they connected with the community. Four intrinsic gratifications were found in the statements shared. Users connected with the community based on the following: Same Behaviors (5), Felt Understood (2), Information Sharing (2), and Confession (1).

Participants who had connected in the groups through finding others who had dealt with the same behaviors allowed the users to know, even without commenting or posting, that their experiences were the realities of many others in the community. "*It's very validating to have a group of people who's like, 'Yeah, I experienced the same things as you.' Even if it's not me commenting, like, 'Hey, I'm experiencing this thing.' Like, like, 'I struggled with this.' It's like, 'Oh yes. Okay. Somebody else has dealt with this as well.'*" The affirmation of same behaviors and lived experiences provided a sense of emotional normalcy for the user. "*It's also good from an emotional point of view to know that there's other people in exactly the same position as you, all over the world. So it's comforting.*" Without the presence of doctors and medical professionals, users felt like they were heard more since it was viewed from a relational perspective.

> *You know, if you're like I am and with the experiences that I've had, you saw a bunch of general doctors and practitioners before you actually went to a psychiatrist who really knows their stuff. And, you know, they throw medication at the problem, perhaps not the dosage or even the medication that you need to actually do anything. And you feel even more, like, despairing over actually feeling any relief, what you're going through. So, being able to go online, find people that are actively going through the things that you're experiencing, and being able to talk to them about it is incredible. It's such a good feeling.*

Medical professionals may not have lived the behaviors at a depth to understand the full experience of their patients or how it impacted their lives.

Overall, the participants found they needed a safe space where individuals could share the same experiences in life without judgment. "*Having a community that's explicitly all these people have this experience, it feels kind of safe there, which I guess is why I'm drawn to them.*" Outside of the communities, there was a fear of judgment. Users did not feel like they could share their own experiences or struggles with friends and family. "*It's just a place to go to feel less like a freak of society as harsh as that sounds. . . . So being able to go somewhere where other people do that too, it's like, okay, great.*" Understanding the experiences is important for all users. As mentioned before, users with similar experiences provided support and understanding for the entire community. A participant shared that they cannot explain the behaviors to friends because they "*felt like a burden to them.*"

Communities also became a central location for information and resources for members. Participants used the community to "*find out more about behaviors*" and applied the findings to their lives. Information could be a variety of different mediums. Valuable information for a user could be "*one line of information*" or items like "*an anxiety diary that somebody else recommended.*"

The community becomes a forum of information that can be applied to users' lives. The different types of posts could create a sense of curiosity where individuals seek more research on a topic. "*Sometimes that* [posts] *can lead you down a path where you do a lot of research yourself and discover something new.*" The act of being vulnerable in a community is something that makes this community unique. Users are focused on sharing their behavioral experiences, but others may view the community as an opportunity for confession. "*It's anonymous, but in a way, you're putting yourself out there, and you're being realized for what you are. There's no hiding.*"

Behavior Focused (n = 6)

It was found that behavior-focused gratifications were not as prominent compared to the other codes. Phase 1 found two codes: Decreased Behaviors (3) and Behavior Modification (3). Decreased behaviors were coded if the participant focused on recovery. Modifications were found when they used the platform for immediate change in currently engaged behaviors such as self-harm or purging. Community members shared the comfort of knowing that "*there's other people in exactly the same position as you, all over the world. So it's comforting.*"

Engagement in the community also provided confidence in situations that once may have been intimidating. "*I think it's decreased a lot of the social anxiety I have. For example, this interview, well, still initially made me pretty anxious 'cause it's, you know . . . it's an unknown. I don't know how it's going to go. I'm at least able to do it now, as opposed to even a few years ago where this would have been impossible for me.*" At the same time, communities offered advice on behaviors but provided a desired avenue for collaborative discourse. "*I usually go on there to just get the thoughts out at the same time. So, I don't know.*"

Online communities offer the gratification of behavior modification as well. If a user engages with behavior, they may seek out assistance through the community. The post of confession or sharing current actions provides a temporal state of hope or a method of coping with the moment. In some cases, advice is given to provide an interruption or modification to the current behavior.

Thematic Coding

In accordance with the literature, the codes were thematically coded in Phase 3. Statements were coded of a main gratification sought in the involvement of the community: Self-confidence (13), Communal Bond (8), Hope (7), and Trust (3).

Self-confidence was the leading gratification found through thematic coding. This theme was found through the engagement between the user and the community. Being able to give back to a community that was helpful in their own behaviors provided a sense of purpose and self-confidence to the user. "*It [the community] gave me feedback on my own problems, but also by giving feedback to other people's problems, it allowed me to feel like I was doing good for the community.*" The giving back to the community mindset allowed users to take on the role of a therapist or a friend. "*So it just kind of goes back to support, like supporting toward better mental health, or better decision-making, improving your health. Sometimes it's just maintaining level with mental health too.*"

Communal bond provides a place of security to gather with others going through the same experiences. "*Being able to go online, find people that are actively going through the things that you're experiencing and being able to talk to them about it is incredible. It's such a good feeling.*" Participants also found a sense of hope through the gratification of finding a listening ear. "*If I want help from somebody, then I can go to Reddit. It's not a counselor, but it has the similar effects, um . . . in an instant sense, just get some recognition and chat to somebody very quickly.*" In addition, a high level of trust was given to the community. Users believed that the moderators and community members were active in providing a helpful community in the platforms studied. Participants sought out informational materials to assist with the behaviors. "*They're helpful in an information sense. I get a lot, lot of good information from, uh, my groups. Even if it's, you know, one line of information, sometimes that can lead you down a path where you do a lot of research yourself and discover something new.*"

Professional Therapy and Online Therapy Communities

The researchers sought to better understand the degree of involvement of participants in professional therapy and online communities. The goal was to gauge the experience of the user with other types of therapy. Often, one may seek help from a variety of resources. The online therapy community becomes one of the various resources that can be used by individuals as they navigate self-damaging behaviors. The majority of the individuals in this research had sought some form of professional therapy with a counselor. About a third sought help in group therapy and more than half had thought about seeking additional help beyond their counselor.

Among those responding to the survey, 114 of the respondents, 73.5 percent, had sought help from a professional counselor at one time or another. Another fifty-one, 32.9 percent, had sought help from a physical form of group therapy. Well over half the respondents, 126/81.3 percent, had talked to a person face-to-face about their behaviors. Some seventy-two respondents, 46.45 percent, did not visit a counselor. Sixty-four of the respondents, 41.3 percent, visited a professional counselor once a week; twelve, 7.7 percent, visited a counselor twice a week; five, 3.23 percent, visited with a counselor three times a week; and two, 1.29 percent, visited a counselor more than four times a week.

Among those surveyed, eighty-eight of the participants, 57.1 percent, had thought about seeking additional help outside of their professional counselor. The majority of respondents, ninety-nine/63 percent, indicated they did not consider the people in their online therapy groups to be their friends (x^2 = 11.29, df = 1, p = 001). A significant number of the respondents, eighty-four/54 percent, reported they sometimes commented in their online community (x^2 = 76.71, df = 4, $p < .001$); thirty-five participants, 22.5 percent, often commented; and twenty-three participants, 14.8 percent, very often commented.

The type of engagement is important in communities. Engagement with online therapy communities was measured in this study by the number of posts and comments that participants would commonly make in a week (see table 6.5). While scrolling through posts in an online therapy community indicated a level of engagement, it lacked the explicitness needed to determine engagement activity. Thus, we considered posts and comments as active engagement. The most common frequency per week was one to three posts and one to three comments. Interestingly, 14.2 percent never posted, but only 2.3 percent never commented. Still, 20 percent of respondents indicated that they commented on posts eleven plus times a week and 14.3 percent posted four to six times a week.

Three Likert statements were used as additional measures to better understand levels of engagement. Using three values, *disagree*, *neutral*, and *agree*, a significant number of respondents, ninety/58 percent, reported that they engaged with online communities every day (x^2 = 52.75, df = 2, $p < .001$). The engagement that occurred was not necessarily with friends; however, ninetey, 58.4 percent, of the participants indicated they did not talk with

Table 6.5 Engagement with Online Groups per Week by Frequency, Percentage, and Chi-Square

Frequency	*Post*	*Comment*
0	18/14.2%	3/2.3%
1–3	71/56.3%**	61/46.9%**
4–6	18/14.3%	16/12.3%
7–10	9/7.1%	24/18.5%
11 plus	10/7.9%	26/20%
Chi-Square	x^2 = 106.93	x^2 = 71.46

N may not always equal 157. *$p < .05$, **$p < .001$.

Table 6.6 Levels of Engagement by Frequency, Percentage, and Chi-Square

Likert Statements	*Disagree*	*Neutral*	*Agree*
I engage with online communities every day.	50/32.3%	15/9.7%	90/58%** x^2 = 52.75
I talk with friends in online communities.	90/58.4%** X^2 = 71.5	31/20.1%	33/21.4%
I talk with strangers in online communities.	63/40.9%	12/7.8%	79/51.38%** x^2 = 46.94

N may not equal 157. p = .01 **df=2.

friends in online communities ($x^2 = 71.5$, df = 4, $p <.001$). But the majority of the participants, seventy-nine/51.3 percent, agreed they talked with strangers in online communities ($x^2 = 46.94$, df = 2, $p < .001$) see (table 6.6).

In the in-depth interviews, two of the participants shared that they were actively engaged in professional therapy. Four had shared that they had participated in professional therapy in the past. While the participants were involved in online communities that provided support, four of the interviewed participants had previous experience with physical support groups or group therapy. Barriers that the participants encountered during the physical groups included lack of engagement/discussion and lack of individual attention. One participant mentioned that the group therapy only dealt with "*hardcore drunk addiction*," but the participant needed support for self-harm. Another participant had to conclude their involvement with therapy because of a change in health insurance.

Though physical support groups are meant to facilitate open communication, participants did not feel like they could be honest. "*There is a fear when you go to therapy that if you say too much, or if you're completely brutally honest about the thoughts that you have in your head, whether or not there's intention behind them, there is a fear that you're going to be locked away and are going to throw the key. You know, 'cause you're going to be committed, or they're going to label you as crazy, or they're going to want to give you all these pills.*" Participants generally felt more open and honest about their experiences online due to the anonymity of the platform. "*I think it's a lot easier to share things in online communities because there's an aspect or anonymity there. In a professional setting, you know, you're speaking directly to a person who is making eye contact with you, and that's difficult.*" Trust was often given blindly to the anonymous platforms without concern for data tracking. "*You're seen, and that information isn't gonna go anywhere.*"

Perceptions of Online Communities

Among the positive aspects of online therapy communities, such as safety, communal bonding, self-confidence, empathy, and reduction in thoughts of self-damaging behaviors, as shown in previous chapters, the researchers realistically expected to find some negative aspects. As much as the therapy communities can help, there are aspects that distract from their purpose. The authors asked participants to share things about their experiences both positive and negative, and this allowed for open conversations. From the data and interview statements provided, online therapy communities are complementary to other forms of care, and members enter with the promise of both providing and finding support among the members. All interview participants promoted the use of the communities and stated they have been useful to themselves and others. However, it would be inappropriate to not address some of the negative aspects that the interview participants shared with us about their experiences with the online therapy communities.

Participants mentioned there is a stigma, at times, that surrounds the online therapy communities. The stigma exists because of societal preconceived ideas of mental health care and because of some inappropriate behaviors. Mental health care takes a back seat to physical care within many health insurance policies. Participants indicated they have sought help within the online communities because their health insurance policies do not cover mental health care. Triggering variables impacted those who struggled with self-harming behaviors and finding societal acceptance in mental health care is as important as physical care, and it continues to evolve. Because of the personal nature of health, privacy is an important factor in being open with health-care providers and with communities where individuals seek help. While anonymity is seen as a positive that allows for more openness within online therapy communities, there exists some fear in these anonymous platforms, as people do not know whom they are talking with.

There are cases where members are exposed to negative posts from parties. Concerns about unwanted sexual messaging were shared by one interview participant, and stories from participants about predatory behaviors across platforms became warning calls for users not to get involved with said communities. "*There's a lot of random sugar daddies that are like, 'Oh, well I'll pay you this much money a week for this and this.' And then there's a lot of people soliciting for sex and a lot of people like trying to sell you drugs.*" Even when users shared their lived experiences with behaviors, unwanted sexual advances were still found. "*It's really hard to tell if some people are being genuine or not, or if they just want to talk to you and be like, 'Okay, now! Can you send me a selfie?'*"

In addition to predatory behavior, some perceptions included encountering monetization schemes in the communities. A participant shared their experiences of a very popular Facebook group focused on anxiety. "*Some people sell their own experience. So they'll post a picture of themselves ten years ago on a page to themselves today. And just say, 'Look at the amazing progress I've made.' Um, 'Come and have a look at my blog,' and their blog leads to a page where you pay them.*" In some cases, users and administrators sell support for other users based on their own experience. The selling party had no therapeutic experience, just a lived experience to provide. "*The guy wanted . . . $6,000 for lifetime support. Um, I don't know how he can possibly give you lifetime support.*"

To formally accept online therapy, the public perception of mental health communities needs to improve. Barriers to engagement are referenced as reasons not to discuss mental health issues online or in person. For example, "*Older generations still shy away from the idea of going to therapy because they think that it means going into an asylum. It's a problem because it's expensive, and people can't afford it.*" In turn, the negative connotations of the mental health conversation have forced users to seek safe spaces that are anonymous, so friends and family will not find the content. In the same way, users felt like they could not be honest with their mental state, with family members, or even with therapists. Participants shared the inner turmoil the behavior secrets had contributed to their own lives. They held a secret that could not be revealed due to the fear of being viewed differently. In addition, the fears of hospitalization or family panic are barriers that prevent honesty in relationships. "*I've definitely seen that on Reddit where people will say, 'I'm having suicidal thoughts, but I'm afraid to tell this to my therapist or a psychiatrist because I'm afraid of being involuntarily hospitalized.' There's probably a better word for it, but they're afraid that the psychiatrist will hospitalize them, and so that's sort of like a type of stigma.*" Participants also shared previous comments from adults who did not understand mental illness and called behaviors "*a phase*." The common vernacular of "*a phase*" is similar to the phrase "*doing it for attention*," often used with self-harm or suicidal thoughts. "*It's something you can do when they're 12 or 13, and they're going through a phase, and it's something that you'll grow out and get over, eventually.*"

While online communities have had their share of negative connotations, they do provide a place for further understanding when people act on behaviors. The resources available could be used by behavior-impacted users or friends of users to obtain information. For example, a participant shared a post they saw recently "'*My suicidal friend stopped communicating. What should I do?' And people will be like, 'Well, you should do a safety check. You should go over there and check on them.' You know? So I feel like in a way it does kind of provide safety resources, but not necessarily in the help line kind of way.*" Conclusions from participants shared that communities can be a negative or positive area, depending on the rules and structure set in place. Without a set of rules to prevent predatory behavior or fiscal-return ploys, members are not protected from toxic behavior. The public perception of communities needs to positively increase to allow others to find the resources they need, which could directly impact the frequency of acted behaviors.

Some social media platforms have taken steps to mitigate issues associated with groups within the platforms. Reporting functions in groups allow users to flag posts or comments that could be offensive or harmful. Reported posts in groups are sent to the group admins for further review. While this is helpful for moderator action, it is dependent on the volunteer-based capabilities of the admins. In addition to reporting, Facebook groups have introduced the ability for anonymous posting, which could allow more openness. This provides users a space to post without having embarrassing questions identified with their own Facebook account. Facebook also has allowed admins to require administrator approval for all posts in groups. This could protect the group and act as a filter for unwanted and toxic posts. Though steps have been taken to provide a safer community, the group relies on the bandwidth of the volunteer administrators. Facebook group activity is a small part of the platform. The distractions of the marketplace, advertisements, newsfeeds, and stories could be distracting for Facebook users. Reddit provides a stronger community connection due to the structure of the platform where administrators log on to monitor their communities and engage in conversation about their self-interest topics. Facebook provides a complex platform that includes topical groups, while Reddit is a platform dedicated to topical groups. Regardless of the platform, group admins may encounter a common concern shared by the participants. The influx of reported posts may be too much for moderators to handle in order to facilitate a safe community.

Online Community Parameters

As is true with various online communities, before a member can participate in a group, they must agree to the terms and guidelines created by the communities in order to become a member. In the case of online therapy communities, guidelines are especially important, as members may have fragile dispositions that could be triggered by inappropriate behaviors, posts, and comments by members. Many of the online groups the researchers contacted to distribute the survey for this study did have guidelines that members had to follow. Among the online therapy community members who granted us permission for interviews, the researchers explored how users defined toxicity in the online communities. This question gathered a contextual understanding of possible harmful effects users could encounter in the communities.

Understanding the toxic behavior users may encounter was important to this study. Based on the responses provided, toxic communities could have very harmful outcomes. Participants shared that toxic communities were locations where "*people tear each other down and more negative responses than positive.*" Participants were advocates of nontoxic communities and shared that to prevent toxicity within the community—uplifting conversations had to be the majority of engagement. However, it was found that toxic traits could be inherited by the admin and moderator team of the community. In one community, a moderator leader scolded other volunteer moderators for not putting enough effort into the community, resulting in a lack of motivation from the interviewed volunteer moderator, in addition to dealing with harmful behaviors. The participant shared this story in a frustrated tone. They were unsure of what they did wrong in their volunteer role while juggling a full-time job. In another case, "*If you don't agree with everything the mod say, and you're not completely into their politics, uh, you'll be banned.*" Toxicity can be facilitated by creating an echo chamber of the moderator's own beliefs. This does not provide a community of desired diversity, honesty, and lived experiences.

Though moderators have power over the community, the users have a list of guidelines to prevent unnecessary conversations. The guidelines may be helpful as a filter for posts, but it still becomes difficult for moderators to stay updated with the influx of posts from larger groups. Participants shared concerns that the number of negative comments can be overwhelming for moderators to filter through and delete. This reporting feature is available to all users and can be used to report harassment or inappropriate conversation. "*They* [the users] *can report it, and that will get sent to us, and they can say why they reported it, or if somebody is harassing them, or whatever the issues be, and then we can see it, and we take care of it, and address it.*" Reporting posts or comments can become overwhelming for a small team of moderators. With the volunteer role of moderators, comments may not receive the attention deserved. Lack of time spent on reported posts could overlook problematic users who continue to post toxic content. Reddit was trusted more regarding guidelines and moderation. One participant shared that Facebook does not have rules in the community they are involved in "*which is probably why it can become quite toxic.*" Facebook groups are a small piece of the platform in comparison to Reddit, where communities are the entire platform. Facebook also has an option in groups that posts have to be approved by moderators; however, comments on posts do not need approval. Admins in Facebook groups may have other responsibilities on the platform where they may forget about the admin duties. This could result in forgotten groups or inactive admins. This was also evident when the researchers reached out to over twenty-five Facebook group moderators in this study and only received one response.

While users did mention that they encounter toxicity, the overall communities they were involved in were focused on behavior modification rather than behavior enabling. One participant stated that the availability of information allowed users to "*see ways in which you can take better care of yourself.*" In contrast, the same user shared, "*Toxic communities that enable bad behaviors are the ones . . . instead of helping you see ways you can take better care of yourself, it helps you see ways in which other people are making it harder for you.*" Toxic communities do not provide a place of honesty but rather a community of fear and judgment.

Behavior modification was promoted due to the presence of other users who were willing to talk about recovery or support. "*If you put up a suicidal post, ideally you're going to have responders that are just like, 'I'm here . . . if you need to talk.' And often, that's just what someone needs who's, you know, feeling very much like that.*" As supported by the leadership roles the participants developed, care is given and obtained through collaborative engagement. Over time, users come together in the behavior-modifying community and share stories of success, behavior interruption, and recovery. The community becomes a very diverse forum, ranging from users previously or currently impacted by self-damaging behaviors.

> *And so you have people who are actively trying to stop the addiction and stop the cycle and stop them from doing that. And so you have people who are giving them tips and tools to help them and telling them this is what worked for me. And then you have the encouragement. I made it seven days, and you get people saying, "Good job!" "Congrats!" Absolutely, people who have made it two years and they get,* [that] *I can come and say that they've made it two years.*

Participants did share responsibility for the community as they took part in the interaction between users; however, a large responsibility was given to the moderators: "*If you're not checking and making sure that what's being posted is appropriate, then it will quickly spiral and you'll get people who will leave who need the help and won't come back because it's become a negative place to be.*" In addition to reviewing posts, users may report or message with concerns about other users. As mentioned before, predatory behavior could be found in the communities that could be dealt with through messaging moderators to ban predatory users. This is another responsibility, in addition to everything else volunteer users are dealing with. If concerns are not addressed timely, public perception is impacted and could lead to negative behavioral impacts.

According to the participants interviewed, toxic characteristics were a mixture of intrinsic feelings and harsh phrasing toward each other. In a toxic environment, users may experience, "*Feelings of blaming others, looking for quick fix solutions rather than really difficult solutions . . . and in toxic communities, they'll sort of promote hopelessness.*" Toxic communities will attract toxic users who "*encourage people to engage in self-defeating behaviors. If someone posts a suicidal post, they'll be like, 'Okay, go do it.'*" If toxic concerns are not addressed by the community and moderators, the group may start to become more behavioral approving and pessimistic. Though not directly toxic, users expressed negative sentiments about paywalls in behavior-focused groups. Users may join a group to seek help but encounter a paywall for help from the moderator team. This was more frequent in Facebook groups where the moderators had identifiable information.

Overall, communities are left to their own community and moderator team to facilitate a safe environment. If users are not protected from toxicity, potential life-threatening outcomes may occur. The engagement that happens online provides distinct positive gratifications or negative implications for each user's life. Communities provide a place where they can be proud of their success. A participant noted at the end of their interview, "*There's no chips. It's not like with Alcoholics Anonymous—you get a 30-day chip or a 60-day chip, or you get like a little ceremony and everything—we don't have that. And so, what we have is a place where you can come and say, 'Hey, I'm really proud of myself. I made it today.'*"

The mixed methodology proved useful to the researchers as they began to examine how the data addressed the hypotheses of this work. Quantitative data is critical to the overall understanding of research questions and hypotheses, and qualitative data allows the researchers to provide greater context to the quantitative data. The multi-pronged approach allowed us to dig deeper, going past reaching a statistical threshold to examine the behaviors, engagements, and self-damaging behaviors. Using appropriate and objective protocol with the qualitative data and the objective use of scales of measurement, the researchers found that all hypotheses were either fully supported by the data or received partial support.

HYPOTHESES

H1: Being engaged with an online support group will decrease thoughts about harmful behaviors.

Hypothesis 1 was partially supported. When this hypothesis was proposed, we used the work of Buglass et al., who suggested "individual's psychosocial well-being, including increases in social support, connectivity, and self-esteem" would help to decrease self-damaging thoughts and behaviors (2017, 248). This decrease would occur even more so when exercised in a group therapy environment, such as a common bond group or online therapy group. We recognized, when proposing that reliance on self-reporting within an online survey, that it might not yield support for this hypothesis nor allow us to make a direct connection to the online therapy group with a decrease in self-damaging behaviors. Nevertheless, it was proposed to help us learn more, whether supported or not. Quantitative data did show that online therapy communities, where respondents engaged, did help them reduce the level of stress in their lives, which could be a trigger among those with self-damaging thoughts or behaviors. A majority of the respondents indicated that their online therapy communities helped them feel better about themselves, and low self-esteem was often identified as a trigger. Respondents indicated these communities helped them get through lonely days and feelings of lack of self-worth, and that the communities helped them navigate their chaotic lives. However, when explicitly asked about whether self-damaging behaviors had decreased, 82.6 percent of respondents indicated self-damaging behaviors were still something they battled with even while in the group. Still yet, the majority believed their recovery had been made easier with the help of their therapy community engagement. And 29 percent of respondents believed their self-damaging thoughts had decreased while being a member of the online therapy community. Thus, using the standard statistical yardstick to support or reject this hypothesis was not enough. Twenty-nine percent believed their self-damaging thoughts decreased, and with this sample, that meant forty-five people found help within their online therapy group, and they found support to get through some of those crises.

The data showed that the therapy communities provided a place of safety and a place to confess behaviors and find support. Through the act of confession and communal bond, a secondary effect of decreased behaviors was supported. Online therapy communities are a place of safety. Qualitatively, we learned that interaction and engagement provided communal bonding, and it is this bonding and support that helped members get through their days. The ability to have anonymity played a critical role in how community members interacted with group members, and they found safety in this anonymous engagement. In most cases, the members were looking for support and even offering support. The ability to discuss with others with similar self-damaging thoughts gave members a rare opportunity to focus on more than their own personal struggles; the community gave the members a place to help others while finding help for themselves. Only people who have dealt with self-harming thoughts can understand the magnitude of the impact these online therapy communities have on their lives.

Often, individuals found the communities by chance as they looked for online help because they could not afford professional help. They could find engagement and community, each of which presented variables that our participants believed were important to their personal well-being. While self-damaging thoughts may not decrease in many, the value of helping just one person makes the online therapy community an important complement to the overall well-being of individuals who regularly live with thoughts of harm. To help those hurting, a holistic approach is needed—each variable added to the care of an individual can provide benefit, and the online therapy communities serve as one of those variables.

Future studies will lead us to measure the longitudinal impact of online therapy communities on individuals. These online therapy communities will evolve over time, and membership will ebb and flow. Quasi-experimental research methodologies should be conducted in the hope of providing more insight into the direct effect of memberships on self-damaging thoughts and behaviors.

H2: Being engaged with an online support group will create feelings of support among the online community.

Hypothesis 2 was fully supported. Individuals have found that social media allows them to develop both physical and digital relationships (Ferris and Hollenbaugh 2018). These virtual relationships help individuals to increase their level of self-esteem and find a sense of belonging. To know someone is there to help you and lift you up is an important part of being a member of any community group. Online therapy communities provide a feeling of support for members.

The findings of this study fully supported feelings of support. Participants stated that they agreed that they felt supported by the online community. In addition, 46.4 percent of participants also shared that they agreed that they felt heard, and 36 percent felt safe in the community. Participants also stated that guidelines protected their well-being, while 35.9 percent proposed that moderators had their best interest in mind. Participants shared that the connection with others provided a support role where they could contribute to others' well-being and feel cared for when needed. The bond of the behaviors created the commonality between users who formed a support network. "*I think sharing my own problems with other people can help them realize that their own problems aren't that weird.*" Community users crafted their own reputations based on previous interactions on the platform linked to their profiles. The feelings of support were founded on the communal bond and trust they had in the community. Guidelines and moderators provided a sense of security for the users.

Question two investigated the motivations sought in using online communities. While 34 percent of participants agreed that they felt safe in identifying online communities, such as Facebook, seventy-four participants strongly agreed they felt safe in anonymous communities, such as Reddit. Support was found not just around the behaviors, but it was a sense of safety. The support is an underlying bond, as users are in the same situation and have bonded together to provide a safe environment. Support is provided by the community members and taken when needed. The relational model provides a support opportunity for topics that have never been revealed in real life.

Seventy-four participants strongly agreed that they discussed topics online that they had not told anyone outside of online relationships. The online community understands the behavior at a deeper level compared to medical professionals. Community members are discussing the lived experiences that resonate with everyone else. It is not a doctor's office where you are treated with medicine or advice. As a participant shared, "*People are there to tell you, you're not alone in what you're experiencing, that they've experienced it as well.*" The ability to find a safe place that is not judgmental was empowering for individuals. "*They're not, they're not judgmental. So I find it very positive. Overall.*"

Users desired a connection more than anything. With isolating behaviors like the ones studied, users can experience loneliness frequently. "*People listen, I've never had anyone, anyone troll me, or put me down.*" Finding a listening body is desired. The act of listening to one's story can provide the feelings of support needed. "*And also just, you know, just being supportive. Yeah, when, when somebody spends time talking, chatting with you on ______, or somebody writes a lengthy response to your lengthy post, you feel like someone is listening and maybe, just then, in itself, can help you feel a little bit more hopeful.*" The platform collaboration of the lived experience as a comment to another user's lived experience post provides users with self-worth and a sense of purpose. "*. . . as long as most people seem to really appreciate and be sort of grateful for your comments, then you feel like, 'Oh yeah, I am! I am doing good for the community.*" This act is unique to the online community. In traditional therapy, the structure is a dyadic conversation with the therapist. The focus is on the individual treated in therapy. However, platform users are able to take on a leadership role and find joy in virtue. As one participant said, "*It's nice being able to just help people.*"

Communities provide the collaborative nature of supporting people seeking not only help but understanding. The goal of the community is to help provide experience and information to the user. Trying to fix the behavior without support or understanding would become painful and traumatic for any user. Users seeking help are not at the stage of recovery. They are looking for a safe place to confide in. A participant stated in the interview a phrase of what the entire community stands for: "*There's no chips. It's not like with Alcoholics Anonymous—you get a 30-day chip or a 60-day chip, or you get like a little ceremony and everything—we don't have that. And so what we have is a place where you can come and say, 'Hey, I'm really proud of myself. I made it today.'*"

OUTLIER FINDINGS

Support is not defined as an elimination of behaviors. As discovered in research question three, sixty-two users (40.3 percent, df = 4, $x^2 = 59.38$) agreed that recovery had been easier thanks to online communities. However, sixty-four users (41.3 percent, df = 4, $x^2 = 54.77$) were neutral that their thoughts of harmful behaviors had decreased since being in the group. In addition, sixty-one (39.4 percent, df = 4, $x^2 = 50.32$) were neutral in that thoughts of harmful behavior had increased since being in the group. Compared to the response of forty users (25.8 percent, df = 4, $x^2 = 19.81$) who strongly disagreed that recovery had been worse due to online communities, the researchers believed support may not have a direct impact on behaviors. It is important to find support through the discovery process of coping, but in order to eliminate or modify behaviors, professional methods should be sought.

> H3: Groups over common bonds, such as a common diagnosis, will create a more connected and supportive group due to common life-impacting situations.

Hypothesis 3 was fully supported. Finding a place where one feels safe and free from judgment is important (Lerman et al. 2017). Because of limitations in health care and insurance that focus on mental health, the online therapy community may serve as a place where similar feelings and behaviors are shared. Mental health issues cut across all generations, all socioeconomic statuses, and all educational levels. Through this common bond of a diagnosis, individuals will seek communities where they hope to be heard. As individuals join online therapy communities, they are acutely aware of the dangers associated with joining a group.

Participants recognized that some groups were not good places to be members and were cognizant of finding groups that had guidelines that members must follow. Participants indicated they liked groups that had moderators in place and genuinely believed that the moderators in the groups were members who did have their best interest in mind, as they served to maintain safety inside the communities. More than 80 percent of respondents indicated that they felt supported in their online therapy communities, and 87 percent felt their behaviors were understood by their online therapy communities.

To find a group that one believes understands his/her diagnosis leads to feelings of trust, and it is this trust that allows members to talk about issues within their virtual community that they have never discussed outside of their digital relationships. With more than 77 percent of the participants indicating that they had found a place where they felt free enough to discuss their thoughts, it is a testament to the online therapy community that enables anonymity and provides the members the freedom to discuss topics that have not been verbalized in other settings. The level of anonymity led members to increase engagement in the communities, and more than 81 percent indicated they felt safe having discussions. Participants indicated that they joined online therapy groups for two primary reasons: companionship and that the groups helped them to feel better. Personal connections are critical to the overall well-being of an individual, and the online therapy communities receive credit for providing needed connections. One participant told the researchers, "*I was just grateful that there was a place that I could go with like-minded people.*" And, another said, "*People are there to tell you, you're not alone in what you're experiencing.*"

H4: Engagement in an online support group will increase emotional openness in social media users.

Finding communities to engage with where one feels safe allows online therapy community members to be more open within the communities. Knowing that one's anonymity is protected provides the necessary support needed to increase levels of engagement and in turn allow for more openness. Most participants in the online surveys indicated that they commonly engaged members in their communities on average of one to three times a week. Fifty-six percent indicated they posted on average one to three times a week, and another 46 percent said they were likely to make comments one to three times a week. Still yet, more people (20 percent) indicated they were likely to comment on others' posts eleven plus times a week. Seeking support less often but providing support more often through comment engagement was supported among those interviewed. As one participant reported and previously stated, "*If I'm just having a bad day, I know I can go in there, and I can affect somebody else, and make them have a better day than what they're having to kind of lift them up. And so, I lift myself up.*"

Finding communities that allow for openness and support and that provides the person affirmation for their willingness to help another increases emotional openness and gives purpose to the seeker of help and those providing help. Establishing this degree of trust provides a community where openness increases and the sharing of information positively impacts those struggling with similar self-damaging thoughts and behaviors. Individuals, who are seeking help regarding sadness, stress, and/or anger, often stumble across online therapy groups in their search for help (Lerman et al. 2017). Curiosity was the prominent factor in the participants' search for groups. They were trying to discover if there were others in similar life situations. The current search results come in the form of digital content, online support groups, and other services. While the results may provide a beneficial result, there is a clear opportunity for users to engage with others over "their experiences and potentially obtain social support" (Lerman 2017, 734).

Chapter 7

Why Online Therapy Communities Matter

The findings from this research do support the value of online therapy communities as a tool to decrease isolation, increase self-confidence, create engagement, and act as a modality that is useful to members, irrespective of the length of time in the group. It is the authors' hope through this research and the awareness of the value of online therapy that communities will increase and individuals struggling will find support. The hope is that individuals, such as those in this study, will be able to speak the words of one of the participants in this research: "*I'm really proud of myself; I made it today.*"

As social media became more integrated into the fabric of people's lives and research emerged showing relationships between mental health and self-harming thoughts, the authors began to explore uses and gratifications as a theoretical tool to examine motivations toward the use of social media platforms and online therapy communities. This theoretical approach led to qualitative and quantitative research in the initial stages that showed that online therapy communities have the potential to help people, leading the authors to expand and refine the research methodologies. It would stand to reason that the use of nonlinear tools (social media platforms) to reach a group of people typically stereotyped with negative "mental health" characteristics provided the researchers with a more robust sample without impacting the participants at the heart of the research work. Collecting thoughts and experiences of people impacted by self-harming thoughts and behaviors as well as learning about membership experiences in online therapy communities led to the discovery of the value of these groups for individuals.

Since mass media was first introduced to this day, studies have been done to better understand the relationship of media with people's behaviors (Bandura 1965; Gerbner 1970). In the 1960s, Congress called for research to examine the relationship between media and violence. This research led to the surgeon general's report in the early 1970s, which did in fact link media to violent behavior toward others and toward self (United States National Institute of Mental Health 1972). At the same time, there have been discoveries that media can be used for learning and to promote positive thoughts and behaviors (Hempstead 2015). Media along with other societal institutions such as family, religion, and education have all been targeted as institutions that have a negative impact on people's behaviors and mental health. Dependent upon any given study, all have been seen as places that either help or harm mental health (Jenson 1990). Sociologists, psychologists, mental health experts, medical doctors, and media specialists have all explored ways to help when people have self-harming thoughts and behaviors.

The authors' expertise as media researchers provides a platform for discovery, and data from this study using the mixed methodology approach suggests that online therapy communities should be used as a tool to combat self-harming thoughts and behaviors. Data from the NIH and the CDC clearly show that self-harming thoughts and behaviors are increasing among the population similar to the sample studied in this research. Many approaches have been used, and the authors believe the findings of this study help to identify another modality that can be used to help people through membership in online therapy communities.

IMPLICATIONS

The findings provide information that may be integrated into holistic care treatments that will aid those with self-harming thoughts and behaviors. The findings have implications for those individuals, their families, caregivers, and society. Media platforms can be used positively to help people by giving individuals tools that cost little, connecting them to online therapy communities where bonding can occur over shared experiences. Communities connected by human empathy, care, and support, provide threads of communal bonding that lead to a reduction of self-harming thoughts and behaviors. In addition, connections can be used for those who find themselves needing support beyond their geographic boundaries. The data supports that people believed that online therapy community members were heard and felt safe within the community. Engagement in therapy communities provided a safe space for individuals who felt as though they could not share behaviors with family or friends. Communities were protected through membership rules that created boundaries around the conversation topic. Through rule establishment, the reputation of the community was formed. User behavior was also guided by rules in the community through clear communication of proper and improper conversations. Each community had different rules created by moderators. There were no standard guides for rules, and rules vary in helpfulness and health for the community. Though based online, these communities break the barriers of time, space, money, and geography. Communities facilitate lasting connections within the group even with the existence of anonymity because anonymous users connect over the behaviors, not over identifying information.

The motivations for engagement in communities include safety, community connection, finding support, giving support, listening, being heard, guidelines, freedom, confession, safety, moderator awareness, anonymity, companionship, and just plain feeling better about oneself. While this is a long list, the data showcases the wide variety of motivations users seek in communities. Users range in personalities and personal needs, which may be why several users need to be heard, yet others want companionship. In the real world, people all have different motivations in their physical communities.

Online community users were motivated within the digital realm by the desire to feel safe and heard by their online connections. These connections created digital threads in a safe place where members could share some of their deepest fears and anxiety. An element of the online community that in some ways is different from a physical community is that there are rules of engagement where members are required to adhere to a certain standard of behavior thus keeping some bad actors out of the community that might otherwise attempt to undermine the connections within the group. While anonymity is often provided as a standard rule within communities, the ability to engage in the community and create lasting connections is still possible among members who remain anonymous. Online communities do what face-to-face therapy groups cannot do—give people without means a much larger community where connections can still be formed.

Finding a connection with others who face self-harming thoughts and behaviors is not easy, whether one lives in a bustling city or a tiny town. There is vulnerability in self-identifying, and stigmas exist. Yet, people are willing to be vulnerable to engage with digital communities where threads of personal connection are possible among members. Among all motivations found—whether it was being heard, staying anonymous from other users, finding companionship, listening, or providing and/or receiving support—all have been based on personal connection. Users sought personal connections online apart from family and friends for fear that they would not understand the topic or that they would judge.

Members recognized their behaviors were not ideal, and they sought digital communities for support. The anonymity allowed users to have relationships with others that were not possible within their physical relationships. The anonymous factor provides less relationship drama compared to identifiable relationships that may put friendships and sometimes family acceptance at risk. Users connected with the presence of diversity, positive feedback, and access to knowledge in the communities. This was a deciding factor in their continuation of engagement in the community. A healthy space does not become an echo chamber of struggles with the presence of the factors mentioned. Diversity, positive feedback, and access to knowledge allowed users to find others on a range of recovery paths that could assist them in their journey. In addition, finding an online community is much like finding a physical community. Users need to find a trustworthy and supportive community. This can be difficult to find a physical and/or online. One must know where to search and what to look for in regard to healthy boundaries. Communities facilitate an environment where members do not feel alone. Users share their own lived experiences of their struggles, which facilitates engagement. Communities seek to provide a place of encouragement, which also provides greater engagement with posts. Higher engagement helps users to feel heard regarding their struggles. The unique combination of lived experience and encouragement is not present in traditional therapy. The dyadic relationship between therapist and patient does not allow that combination; however, the online community thrives on that model. In addition to the thriving model, the asynchronous interaction groups present opportunities for members to find help among archival interactions between users.

The community can have positive and negative effects on the user. Behaviors may be modified with the assistance of community members and by encountering lived experiences. Such events have allowed users to pursue recovery or decrease the frequency of self-damaging events. Communities have also been used to interrupt behaviors. Users may write suicide letters or describe their active moments of self-harm in the communities. Encountering a community on the platform at a crucial moment may assist in interrupting the behavior acted upon at that moment.

However, the communities may breed toxic environments through behavior that encourages negative or predatory posts. The encouragement of behaviors does not provide recovery or modification for users seeking to reduce their behaviors. Toxic communities may provide encouragement or instruction for self-harming behaviors and even suicidal thoughts. However, instructions are sought in other communities to discover how to engage with behaviors in a safe way. Users in self-harm communities have asked how to engage in behaviors in a way that is not life threatening. In some cases, this is due to the moderator's comfortability with the topic. Toxic communities provide an acceptance of the behavior without striving to modify engaged behaviors.

Online therapy community members come into the communities with different needs: some for discussion, others for interruption, and others for communal bonding and confession without judgment. A healthy community provides leadership opportunities for users in all stages of behavior recovery.

Members may assume leadership roles as moderators after receiving help within the group. Members may come and go, but the stabilizing nature of moderators with firsthand experiences within the group yield richer opportunities to help new members. Leaders in the community provide shepherding through posts. Some posts are likely to receive greater interaction than others due to various factors. Leaders may emerge on posts and comments to ensure that the body of the whole feels heard. Empathy plays a vital role among members, as they all have had their own lived experiences with the topics discussed.

Users are influenced by a variety of motivations. With the rise of mental health issues, online communities are helpful in providing a place of support regardless of the motivation sought. The interpersonal connection allows users to bond over behaviors and find others struggling with the same issues. Online communities were very helpful in moments where physical connection seemed impossible. For example, people gravitated to online communities during the COVID-19 lockdowns due to isolation. Users sought digital personal connection with others when the ability to connect in the physical world was limited.

The data supports that personal connection creates an environment of care within the online therapy community. The most personal of struggles often lead individuals to connections apart from family and friends. These connections are sought due to feelings of lack of understanding. The findings remind us that an online community is much like finding a physical community. Seeking a community where one feels the support needed is never easy. Searching for a trustworthy and supportive community takes time and finding a community where one can trust someone is important. Online communities remove standards and can provide anonymity, allowing for people to have relationships without judgment within the online community. Feelings of being alone can fade with engagement in online communities and can lead to greater engagement among members. Even relationships with family and friends can improve as online communities help to improve members' feelings of self-worth. In addition, because online relationships do not necessarily breed relationship drama, this too may help members with relationships outside the digital communities. Gaining knowledge that helps online members to cope is valuable to digital and nondigital community members. Access to a diverse group of individuals provides members with diverse coping skills and positive feedback that can enhance self-esteem. Sharing lived experiences and knowledge leads to community engagement, and engagement can lead to improved mental and physical health.

Asynchronous interaction is a benefit that allows others to explore archival interactions. Learning about ways that people cope with self-harming behavior and how to interrupt thoughts of self-harm is an important feature of the online therapy community. Yet, real-time interruption is extremely important as well. Often, real-time interaction and engaged members can create a thread of interruption that is needed by another member, and this interruption can walk a member back from engaging in the self-harming behavior. Communal bonding and confession without judgment are important variables in the recovery or maintenance of health behaviors and the ability to function in physical communities beyond online relationships. Moderators often provide online therapy communities with the wisdom and care that is needed to shepherd members through rough experiences. Good shepherding happens within online therapy communities. Some posts are likely to receive greater interaction than others. Empathy plays a role among members, where leaders may emerge in some cases to ensure that the body of the whole community feels heard.

While engagement within the community does not create an immediate recovery response, users seek and find support through engagement. While online communities play an important part in the recovery process, the combination of other modalities should be included to find full recovery. Often, users sought online communities out of curiosity. Participants shared that they believed they were the only people dealing with the behaviors until they found the community. The engagement allowed the discovery of a large population dealing with the same behaviors. This provided a group effort rather than a solo journey of making sense of the behaviors. The immediate ability to discuss with someone when behaviors were triggered was empowering for all users, which made recovery easier. Users may even find resources to assist with recovery.

A gratification emerged with the ability to provide support in the community. Users created a digital ecosystem of giving and taking support when needed. Days might come when users are impacted heavily, and they seek support, but the next day they may be providing the same support to others when others encounter similar challenges. Users may even share methods they learned from their own authored posts. The community allowed users to share secrets and behaviors without feelings of judgment. Furthermore, the anonymity gave users the freedom to feel safe when discussing behaviors, which mitigated the risk of the behaviors connected to their own identity. However, an important perspective to remember is that the change of behaviors is not the responsibility of the community or other members. Behavior change remains the user's responsibility. They may find support, engagement, and encouragement, but without the desire to let gratification findings impact the behaviors in addition to professional therapy, one may not find full recovery.

While 57 percent stated that they were still impacted by behaviors, members found that just knowing others had similar experiences helped with processing their own lives. Some members weren't comfortable posting about their experiences, nor were they willing to engage with others through comments, but still seeing the interaction among other members helped those to recognize that their own realities were similar to others, and thus they found validation from vicarious exposure to other member engagements. While communities did not have a direct connection with a decrease or increase in behaviors, users found increased confidence and a communal bond in the membership. The bond one had in the group provided safety and trust, gratifications that users may not have received elsewhere. The groups can impact individuals, but the significance of that support must be measured in combination with other modalities designed to help in each person's treatment and care. It is important to note and reemphasize that being within the group does not preclude someone from being impacted by self-damaging behaviors, but it does give members opportunities to seek support, find empathy, and it can make recovery easier. The opportunity to be a supporting member of an online community instead of a receiving member was the highest gratification among in-depth interview participants. This was not a gratification the authors considered when developing the data collection instruments. Doing good for the community is an important gratification. Community members find that just knowing that others have similar experiences helps members deal with their self-damaging behaviors. Increased confidence in oneself is created with the help of the online community members who help other members navigate situations that in the past may have been intimidating.

It should be noted that a majority of participants in this work have discussed their behaviors face-to-face or with a professional counselor. However, users felt safer under the trust of anonymity. The non-identified account or lack of physical presence allowed for a deeper explanation without relationship bias interfering with the discussion. However, it was not found that participants were able to recover through online communities only. A combination of professional therapy and online communities provided the professional treatment and community connection one may need for a full recovery.

Online therapy communities serve as a complement to a variety of modalities. Almost 75 percent of all respondents had seen a professional counselor, another 81 percent had talked to someone face-to-face about their behaviors, and more than 50 percent had thought about seeking extra help beyond their counselors. What the online community allowed for was a more open and honest discussion of experiences compared to a physical group. The diversity of user membership allowed users to encounter a wide range of behavioral experiences. The volume of active users and frequency of posts resulted in greater engagement compared with physical support groups. Users were not limited to hearing about the experiences of a physical support group just of fifteen to twenty people. Community members read posts from across the globe and received countless comments about advice and experiences. In addition to reading posts, participants posted one to three times on average, 14 percent posted four to six times, 7 percent posted seven to ten times, and almost 8 percent posted more than eleven times a week. The authored posts allowed users to receive custom-tailored guidance for their own behaviors. Apart from posting, more than 50 percent of users would comment on posts four to eleven plus times a week. For half of the group, contact with group members occurred just about every day in this study. These comments suggest a strong desire among members to provide support to others in their ongoing battles with behaviors. Greater engagement with individuals may occur more readily in online communities than in physical support groups because there are more people to engage with than in a physical community. Anonymity allows for a more open and honest discussion of experiences within the online community compared to a physical group.

Data for this study was collected during the COVID-19 pandemic. The authors would be remiss if we did not address the impact of the 2020 COVID-19 pandemic and the impact this unprecedented occurrence had on people's perceptions of digital communities. For it was the 2020 COVID pandemic that legitimized the power of the digital community. When communal bonding and physical contact were taken from individuals and as lockdowns were implemented to interrupt the transmission of the deadly COVID-19 virus, people used online tools to create opportunities to maintain relationships and even to develop new relationships. The presence of the new digital connection communities and the acceptance of the technology to remain bonded enhanced the legitimacy of making digital connections that served to create inclusion and engagement, and thus increased people's acceptance of digital communities for a variety of purposes, including online therapy communities that help people with self-harming thoughts and behaviors.

For those in online communities dedicated to self-damaging behaviors, users were aware of the risks and benefits of the communities. While there were negative aspects mentioned, the benefits greatly outweighed the risks of engagement. Such risks of predatory behavior, fiscal motivations of moderators, and other issues have created a negative stigma among the online communities. It is important to note that stigma is not founded on the community and potential recovery of behavior. Stigma is created based on the fear of who users may be engaging with. Anybody can create an account and create a false narrative on the platform, which has been included in mainstream news about social media cautions. In addition to user caution, users should be cautious about the health of the community. Communities should be evaluated just as anybody would do with a physical group. Such communities could become toxic if not moderated quickly.

Moderators must be active in learning the changes to the platforms and actively responding to issues in the community. If moderators become inactive, users are left on their own. The ability to maintain a large community with volunteer administrators is a feat to be admired. That feat is fueled by their own behavior stories where they found value in the community, and they desired to help people see that same value.

The data supports that the positive aspects of online therapy communities outweighed the negative aspects. A negative stigma for mental health care exists among professional caregivers and online therapy communities. Finding positive communities is much like finding positive groups in physical settings. Caution within online therapy communities must be present. Just like getting to know a physical group of people, the online community evolves and develops. For all the good coming from online therapy communities, there are cases where inappropriate behaviors exist.

Social media platforms change rules for groups and members. Rule changes within social media platforms make managing groups better in some cases, but not always easier or safer in other cases. Ultimately, it often comes down to the ability of the group moderators and members to ensure that the group is a place of safekeeping and care.

In healthy communities, companionship is found around the topic of behaviors. In most groups, behavior modification is the goal. The groups are not in place to enable a behavior but are there to help group members with behavior modification. The hope is that self-damaging thoughts will not be acted on, and the online therapy community members play a role in providing engagement to members in the moment when thoughts are triggered. While the quantitative data showed that participants still dealt with self-damaging thoughts and behaviors, 29 percent believed these thoughts and behaviors were reduced, and for that, the online therapy communities receive some credit. Users sought out online communities due to the issues of accessibility for professional therapy. Lack of health insurance coverage and costly online options were not accessible to many individuals. In some groups, a paywall was found for additional support from moderators or for exclusive access to a deeper community. This was in addition to the basic community that the user was engaged in. Promises of "lifetime support" were proposed to create consumer conversions with the paywall.

Groups have established rules to prevent unnecessary conversation and content that may be triggering for some. If users break rules, they could be given a warning or be banned from the group. Moderators only know about problematic behavior if they encounter it from a user's perspective or through the reporting feature in the communities. When posts are reported, they are sent to the moderators for review. However, the moderators are volunteers with responsibilities outside of the group. A large volume of reports could become overwhelming for a small team of moderators that receives no financial compensation for their time. This could be triggering for them as well since they have engaged in behaviors at some point. Original posters can be monitored, and posts may need to be approved by a moderator, but comments related to the original post do not need approval. Finding a community to help with self-damaging thoughts and behaviors is difficult. Many seek these groups because of financial barriers; some find some online groups that create paywalls after first entry into the groups. Granted, moderators must spend a great deal of time moderating groups, and this time takes them away from other jobs where they receive payment. Another concern is that these moderators, while trained in managing a group, may not have the necessary training to offer the level of support that some members would expect if a paywall were part of being in the group.

While online support groups were beneficial for users, they did not decrease thoughts about harmful behavior, but they did provide communal bonding. Communities provided other factors that could be used as an introduction to recovery. Stress was found to be a trigger for thoughts and behaviors. Communities provided a safe environment that assisted with stress reduction. Through engagement in the community, users felt better about themselves knowing that they were not alone in their behaviors. The unique communities provided various gratifications that were important to users: confession, support, and communal bond.

Communities have provided an opportunity for community members to learn more about behaviors without the fear of health insurance or monetary barriers. Though behaviors were not significantly diminished as a result of the group engagement, the ability to find a connection was important for users. As users understand behaviors more through encountering lived experiences and communal bonds, they may be more open to receiving the answers they desire from within the community. Online therapy communities help people feel better about themselves, get through their good and bad days, provide a platform to confess behaviors, create greater connections among more people, and supply support when monetary barriers exist to getting care. Using online therapy communities as part of a holistic approach where multiple modalities are employed is part of a pathway to better care for those who struggle with self-damaging thoughts and behaviors.

Community support was found to be prevalent in the groups. Through careful moderation and rule establishment, users found feelings of safety. The ability to stay anonymous provided a more engaging group without the fear of relationship turmoil. Users felt that the support found was based on the understanding of others with similar behaviors. The providing and taking support were based on listening and empathy, which is a gratification users may not receive in physical relationships. The combination of online support and professional counseling provides both community/understanding and professional opinion. Combined care methods would work best in handling the questions individuals may seek answers to. Furthermore, moderated online therapy communities with professional counselors may prove most effective. Empathy helps when communicating with group members about self-damaging behaviors, and knowing someone is listening is an important engagement tool within the online therapy communities that creates opportunities for healing and helping. Combined care methods work best using professional counseling and online therapy communities.

Groups sharing common bonds, such as a common diagnosis, will create a more connected and supportive group due to common life-impacting situations. Users found trust, which resulted in sharing lived experiences without any concern about relationship repercussions. When experiences were shared, users found countless others willing to listen to their own rants, behaviors, triggers, stories, and more. Users finding other people willing to listen to topics that were often kept hidden from physical relationships were gratifying to the community seeker. As trust was established, other users became online friends who built on messages and engagement with one another. Being heard is an important variable in finding an online therapy community that can help individuals who are dealing with self-damaging behaviors. To believe someone is listening is important, but to be heard goes beyond mere listening. Trust is fragile and so important to the online therapy participant. Trust leads to engagement, and engagement leads to companionship. A personal connection decreases feelings of being alone.

Engagement in an online support group will increase emotional openness in social media users. The act of confession and sharing discussions they have not told anyone else provides a place of openness and safety. They do not recognize friends or strangers in the community but seek a place of safety. Similar to the act of confession in the Catholic Church, users find a place of confession through anonymity (confessional booth). Users share confessions and stories with trusted members (priests) and receive instructions or advice (penance). The ability to communicate and share openly helps community members get help with feelings of sadness, stress, and even anger.

Chapter 8

Conclusion

We introduced the reader to the goals of community therapy in chapter 4. Our data show that motivations and gratifications of face-to-face community therapies can similarly be found among online therapy community members. Thus, we believe online therapies can be a therapy of choice, not necessarily a replacement for face-to-face community therapies, but one that provides some of the same advantages.

Finding a place where communal bonding is available for those who seek it can be difficult for people who live with self-harming behaviors. People seek communities where they can bond with the positives and negatives in their lives. A person looks for places where he/she can find empathy and support. They seek out those who can celebrate with them when good things happen, so when things get difficult, support is provided. Engaging with a supporting community is often made hard with financial constraints, geographical distance, and the lack of empathy from those geographically close. Online therapy communities can be used to remove some of these barriers. Online communities are formed over common characteristics among members. For those who deal with self-harming thoughts and behaviors, the online community can provide a safe space for communal bonding and support.

Community connection is a major motivation for people as they seek out online therapy communities. Finding someone who struggles with the same self-damaging behavior and discovering that those individuals exist removes the feelings of isolation as people address their own thoughts of self-damage.

Within the online therapy communities, sharing lived experiences and the knowledge learned from those experiences leads to greater community engagement. When community members are able to communicate with others and feel safe doing so, the individual members become more engaged and comfortable sharing struggles and connecting with others on the same topic.

These connections lead to opportunities to help members modify behaviors and even interrupt impending self-harming behaviors. This engagement can lead to feelings of belonging and of making a difference in the lives of other community members.

An important aspect of the online therapy community is user protection. Finding a safe space where people listen to members and provide empathy and support under an umbrella of kindness is the hope of most people as they seek to engage communities. Knowing that one's thoughts are shared by other people beyond themselves helps members become more confident and safe as they make new connections inside the online therapy communities. Making the online therapy community safe lies with the membership. Moderators do set group guidelines and rules. Maintaining a community where guidelines are followed can, at times, be a full-time job. Moderators do have the latitude to make rules and determine if members should be removed.

Dialogue is critical to the success of online therapy communities. Dialogue can be nurtured and flourished when communities provide safe spaces for honest discussion and interaction. The ability to remove comments that create discomfort is important. Anonymous communities must be proactive in reporting harmful content. Guidelines must be enforced for the sake of safety. Ensuring that trolls are not allowed in and that trigger-sensitive content is not present is all part of making the community a safe space. Communities with large membership will be most successful when the duties of the moderator are shared among several in the membership. Longtime members who ultimately begin to take on roles as mentors within groups can become some of the best moderators as they have empathy for members and understand triggering content that can be harmful to new and even more seasoned members. With member investments in online therapy communities, communal bonding is possible.

Personal connection is a primary gratification that members report seeking within the online therapy communities. Finding a space with no judgment is an important characteristic hoped for when in search of community.

People join groups because they seek connections that provide listening, provide positive feedback, and are behavior focused. When a physical community cannot provide the listening, is not willing to provide positive feedback, and is unwilling to focus on the behavior instead of the person, individuals can find support among online therapy community members who are willing to meet the needs for personal connection. There are times when friends and family cannot meet the needs of a person dealing with self-damaging behaviors, and there are times when professional counselors are unable to meet the needs of those with the same damaging behaviors and thoughts. It is during these times that the online therapy community can play a critical role in the overall care of an individual. Providing interruptions in negative self-damaging behaviors is an important role that community members share with those they engage with. Knowing that someone is listening is important within communities. The added value of anonymity provides a safe space.

Online therapy communities may be able to provide the resources needed to help with recovery. Group members can share help beyond listening. Finding online therapy communities can be a struggle. Participants in this study reported that they stumbled upon communities out of curiosity. Often, feeling alone and having difficulty accepting oneself led members to search for help beyond the traditional modalities of professional counselors, physical support groups, family, and friends. While what leads each person to a community is varied, participants in this study gave partial credit to the online therapy communities for their own recovery.

As we explored reasons for joining, we also looked for a reason for continuing to be a part of an online therapy community. Community connection allows longer invested members the opportunity to provide help to new members, and the archival nature of the online therapy community allows members to review previous discussions that may be impactful to new members. Knowing that one's struggles may have passed and that same struggle shared in previous postings and the engagement with other community members at that time helps someone else is a morale booster and helps confirm the self-worth of long-standing community members.

Leaders within the online therapy communities emerge over time. Studying long-standing members and the roles they play should be examined in the future. These leaders often emerge when they see that some of the posts for members seeking help lack the engagement needed to mitigate issues with new and old members. These leaders emerge to provide the engagement needed to help members. Having someone acknowledge a post through a like or comments can make a difference in how the members perceive an overall online community. Being present and actively commenting on users' posts are characteristics of emerging community leaders. Some may offer advice and share experiences; others emerge by listening. It is the characteristic of listening that often helps members.

Common concerns did emerge regarding the fear of being identified within online therapy communities. Knowing that identity is protected allows for deeper sharing of thoughts of self-harm and behaviors. Protection of identity and protection of self were expressed as participants worried about future job opportunities and social relationships. Participants admitted to being fearful of outsiders connecting them to real-world identities that could impact economic well-being. Some indicated that while they served as mental illness counselors outside of the online community, they too still struggled with their own self-damaging thoughts and behaviors and used the online therapy community as a space to address their personal struggles. Others indicated that they feared their families would learn about their own struggles, and the online therapy communities provided the engagement needed to protect themselves.

An important aspect of the online communities was the ability for the space to provide a place for different stages of the behavior. Recovery is important, and longevity in the community may allow for members to successfully engage with family and friends regarding behaviors as time passes. The willingness of members to invest time and support within an online therapy community showed that members did expect to find hope and recovery within the group. As previously mentioned, users may not seek help with behaviors as much as they seek to understand if they are alone in their struggles.

The online therapy community is a collaboration of members providing support, giving advice, and actively engaging with other members. While individuals in this research still dealt with self-damaging thoughts and behaviors as members of the online therapy communities, 40 percent felt the recovery was made easier by being a member of the community, and another 29 percent believed self-harming thoughts had decreased since becoming a member of the online community. Knowing a member may have helped users with recovery as the connection acted as a motivation for staying in the group. This personal connection to others' recovery was important to members, and the idea of "*doing good for the community*" provided affirmation of community membership for support providers. With behavioral limitations, members find a sense of freedom and purpose from community engagement. The ability to be vulnerable in this type of community is important. There will be times when members use the community to confess thoughts and behaviors. And it is during these times that listening and engaging with the member in crisis can help that member through that journey. Through the engagement, confidence can increase and thoughts of self-damage can decline. Confession or sharing current actions can provide hope and a method of coping in the moment. During these moments, behavior interruptions can occur. Behavior change goes beyond the online therapy communities, and the discussion of mental health issues must be normalized for care to occur.

Negative connotations toward mental health led people to seek help from online therapy communities. Participants shared the inability to have conversations with people about their thoughts contributed to their self-harming behaviors. The ability to share the secrets within the online therapy community allowed them to avoid being viewed differently by family and friends.

For the therapy community to be a safe space, it must be a nontoxic community. Engagement must be positive and supportive. Shared guidelines must be followed, and multiple moderators are important elements of a supportive online therapy community. Communities must listen and engage members and support behavior modification and behavior interruptions.

Behavioral change ultimately is the responsibility of the individual members of an online community. Members are not responsible for others to change behaviors; it remains the original poster. However, members did indicate that supportive engagement was useful in helping members avoid self-damaging behaviors. Gathering information from the online community is an important element of care. Being provided with information that increases one's knowledge of care options is important. The online therapy community is a modality that can be used when no other treatment options are available.

Lack of health-care insurance and fear of leaving home were all barriers to getting treatment. The online therapy community led by members and moderators can be used to reduce the barriers to receiving care. Knowing that others deal with the same challenges helps users to find engaging communities that provide the support needed to progress toward recovery. While medical professionals are often needed, the ability to pay can keep a person from receiving this help. It is then that the online therapy community and its members can stand in as support when no other support is possible. The hope will be another community member, another person, a friend, a family member who will be able to say, "*I'm really proud of myself. I made it today.*"

References

ADAA. 2021. "Facts." *Anxiety and Depression Association of America.* Accessed June 18, 2021. https://adaa.org/understanding-anxiety/facts-statistics.

Albrecht, Terrance L., and Mara B. Adelman. 1987. "Communicating Social Support: A Theoretical Perspective." In *Communicating Social Support*, edited by Terrance L. Albrecht and Mara B. Adelman, 18–39. Beverly Hills: Sage.

Alexa Internet, Inc. 2022. "Top Sites in United States: By Country." *Alexa.* https://www.alexa.com/topsites/countries/US.

Ambrose, Charles T. 2011. "Joseph Hersey Pratt, M.D.: The Man Who Would Be Osler." *Microbiology, Immunology, and Molecular Genetics Faculty Publications* 44 (11). https://uknowledge.uky.edu/cgi/viewcontent.cgi?article=1044&context=microbio_facpub.

Anderson, Benedict. 2016. *Imagined Communities: Reflections on the Origin and Spread of Nationalism.* Rev. ed. London; New York: Verso.

Anderson, Monica, and Jingling Jiang. 2018. "Teens' Social Media Habits and Experiences." *Pew Research Center.* Published November 28, 2018. Accessed July 16, 2021. https://www.pewresearch.org/internet/2018/11/28/teens-social-media-habits-and-experiences/.

Anderson, Monica, and Jingling Jiang. 2018a. "Adolescents, Social Media, & Technology 2018." *Pew Research Center.* https://www.pewresearch.org/internet/2018/05/31/adolescents-social-mediatechnology-2018/.

Apple. 2022. "Whisper—Share, Express, Meet." Apple Apps Preview: Whisper Text LLC, Apple, Inc. March 16, 2022. https://apps.apple.com/us/app/whisper-share-express-meet/id506141837.

Arrington, Michael. 2006. "It's Official(ish): Myspace Is Biggest Site on Internet | TechCrunch." *Tech Crunch*, December 12, 2006. https://techcrunch.com/2006/12/12/its-officialish-myspace-is-biggest-site-on-internet/.

ASFP. 2019. "Suicide Statistics." *American Foundation for Suicide Prevention*, June 22, 2019. https://afsp.org/suicide-statistics/.

Aubrey, Jennifer Stevens, and Leslie Rill. 2013. "Investigating Relations between Facebook Use and Social Capital among College Undergraduates." *Communication Quarterly* 61 (4): 479–496. https://doi.org/10.1080/01463373.2013.801869.

Auxier, Brook, and Monica Anderson. 2021. "Social Media Use in 2021." *Pew Research Center: Internet, Science & Tech,* April 7, 2021. https://www.pewresearch.org/internet/2021/04/07/social-media-use-in-2021/.

Bandura, Albert. 1965. "Influence of Models' Reinforcement Contingencies on the Acquisition of Imitative Responses." *Journal of Personality and Social Psychology* 1 (6): 589. https://doi.org/10.1037/h0022070.

Barak, Azy, Meyran Boniel-Nissim, and John Suler. 2008. "Fostering Empowerment in Online Support Groups." *Computers in Human Behavior* 24 (5): 1867–1883. https://doi.org/10.1016/j.chb.2008.02.004.

Bar-Lev, Shirly. 2008. "'We Are Here to Give You Emotional Support': Performing Emotions in an Online HIV/AIDS Support Group." *Qualitative Health Research* 18 (4): 509–521. https://doi.org /10.1177 /1049732307311680.

Bell, Vaughan. 2007. "Online Information, Extreme Communities and Internet Therapy: Is the Internet Good for Our Mental Health?" *Journal of Mental Health* 16 (4): 445–457. https://psycnet.apa.org/doi/10.1080/09638230701482378.

Binder, Matt. 2019. "No, Facebook Isn't Getting Rid of Your Secret Group." Mashable, Inc., August 14, 2019. https://mashable.com/article/facebook-secret-groups-private-hidden/.

Blumler, Jay G. 1979. "The Role of Theory in Uses and Gratifications Studies." *Communication Research* 6 (1): 9–36. https://doi.org/10.1177/009365027900600102.

Børøsund, Elin, Milada Cvancarova, Shirley M. Moore, Mirjam Ekstedt, and Cornelia M. Ruland. 2014. "Comparing Effects in Regular Practice of E-Communication and Web-Based Self-Management Support among Breast Cancer Patients: Preliminary Results from a Randomized Controlled Trial." *Journal of Medical Internet Research* 16 (12): e295. lled trial. https://doi.org/10.2196/jmir.3348.

Bouchard, Stéphane, Belle Paquin, Richard Payeur, Micheline Allard, Vicky Rivard, Thomas Fournier, Patrice Renaud, and Judith Lapierre. 2004. "Delivering Cognitive-Behavior Therapy for Panic Disorder with Agoraphobia in Videoconference." *Telemedicine Journal and E-Health* 10 (1): 13–25. https://doi.org/10.1089/153056204773644535.

Bourdieu, Pierre. 1986. "The Forms of Capital." In *Handbook of Theory and Research for the Sociology of Education*, edited by John G. Richardson, 241–258. Westport: Greenwood Press.

Braithwaite, Dawn O., Vincent R. Waldron, and Jerry Finn. 1999. "Communication of Social Support in Computer-Mediated Groups for People with Disabilities." *Health Communication* 11 (2): 123–151. https://doi.org/10.1207/s15327027hc1102_2.

Brandtzæg, Petter Bae. 2012. "Social Networking Sites: Their Users and Social Implications—A Longitudinal Study." *Journal of Computer-Mediated Communication* 17 (4): 467–488. https://doi.org/10.1111/j.1083-6101.2012.01580.x.

Brint, Steven. 2001. "Gemeinschaft Revisited: A Critique and Reconstruction of the Community Concept." *Sociological Theory* 19 (1): 1–23. https://doi.org/10.1111/0735-2751.00125.

Brown, Brené, Katy Davis, Abi Stephenson, and Al Francis-Sears. 2013. "Brené Brown on empathy." Film by RSA, Uploaded December 10, 2013, 2:53. YouTube video. https://www.youtube.com/watch?v=1Evwgu369Jw.

Brown, John Seely, and Paul Duguid. 2000. *The Social Life of Information*. Boston: Harvard Business Publishing.

Brownstein, Ronald. 2015. "How Has Technology Changed the Concept of Community?" *The Atlantic*, October 10, 2015. https://www.theatlantic.com/technology/archive/2015/10/community-in-the-digital-age/408961/.

Buglass, Sarah L., Jens F. Binder, Lucy R. Betts, and Jean D. M. Underwood. 2017. "Motivators of Online Vulnerability: The Impact of Social Network Site Use and FOMO." *Computers in Human Behavior* 66: 248–255. https://doi.org/10.1016/j.chb.2016.09.055.

Bury, Michael. 1982. "Chronic Illness as Biographical Disruption." *Sociology of Health and Illness* 4 (2): 167–182. https://doi.org/10.1111/1467-9566.ep11339939.

Cacioppo, John T., James H. Fowler, and Nicholas A. Christakis. 2009. "Alone in the Crowd: The Structure and Spread of Loneliness in a Large Social Network." *Journal of Personality and Social Psychology* 97 (6): 977. https://doi.org/10.1037/a0016076.

Calancie, Olivia, Lexi Ewing, Laura D. Narducci, Salinda Horgan, and Sarosh Khalid-Khan. 2017. "Exploring How Social Networking Sites Impact Youth with Anxiety: A Qualitative Study of Facebook Stressors among Adolescents with an Anxiety Disorder Diagnosis." *Cyberpsychology: Journal of Psychosocial Research on Cyberspace* 11 (4). https://doi.org/10.5817/CP2017-4-2.

Carey, James W. 1989. *Communication as Culture*. New York; London: Routledge.

Cater, Douglass, and Stephen Strickland. 1975. "TV Violence and the Child: Evolution and Fate of the Surgeon General's Report." *Russell Sage Foundation*. Retrieved July 16, 2021. http://www.jstor.org/stable/10.7758/9781610446006.

Chamberlin, J. 2004. "Survey Says: More Americans Are Seeking Mental Health Treatment." *Monitor on Psychology* 35 (7): 17. https://www.apa.org/monitor/julaug04/survey.

Chen, Jenn. 2022. "Instagram Statistics You Need to Know for 2022." *Sprout Social*. March 15, 2022. https://sproutsocial.com/insights/instagram-stats/.

Chen, Liang, and Jingyuan Shi. 2015. "Social Support Exchanges in a Social Media Community for People Living with HIV/AIDS in China." *AIDS Care* 27 (6): 693–696. https://doi.org/10.1080/09540121.2014.991678.

Chen, Yixin, and Yang Xu. 2021. "Exploring the Effect of Social Support and Empathy on User Engagement in Online Mental Health Communities." *International Journal of Environmental Research and Public Health* 18 (13): 6855. https://doi.org/10.3390/ijerph18136855.

Chung, Jae Eun. 2013. "Social Interaction in Online Support Groups: Preference for Online Social Interaction over Offline Social Interaction." *Computers in Human Behavior* 29 (4): 1408–1414. https://doi.org/10.1016/j.chb.2013.01.019.

Clark, Jenna L., Sara B. Algoe, and Melanie C. Green. 2018. "Social Network Sites and Well-Being: The Role of Social Connection." *Current Directions in Psychological Science* 27 (1): 32–37. https://doi.org/10.1177/0963721417730833.

Cobb, Nathan K., Amanda L. Graham, and David B. Abrams. 2010. "Social Network Structure of a Large Online Community for Smoking Cessation." *American Journal of Public Health* 100 (7): 1282–1289. https://doi.org/10.2105/ajph.2009.165449.

Cobb, Nathan K., Amanda L. Graham, M. Justin Byron, and David B. Abrams. 2011. "Online Social Networks and Smoking Cessation: A Scientific Research Agenda." *Journal of Medical Internet Research* 13 (4): e119. https://doi.org/10.2196/jmir.1911.

Corbin, Juliet M., and Anselm L. Strauss. 1987. "Accompaniments of Chronic Illness: Changes in Body, Self, Biography, and Biographical Time." *Research in the Sociology of Health Care* 9: 249–281. https://doi.org/10.4135/9781446260883.

Davis, Katie, David P. Randall, Anthony Ambrose, and Mania Orand. 2015. "'I Was Bullied Too': Stories of Bullying and Coping in an Online Community." *Information, Communication & Society* 18 (4): 357–375. https://doi.org/10.1080/1369118X.2014.952657.

Dennis, Everette E., and Melvin L. DeFleur. 2010. *Understanding Media in the Digital Age*. New York: Allyn & Bacon.

Douglas, Heather. 2010. "Community, Types of." In *International Encyclopedia of Civil Society*, edited by Helmut K. Anheier and Stefan Toepler, 539–544. New York: Springer. https://doi.org/10.1007/978-0-387-93996-4_542.

Dunbar, Michael S., Lisa Sontag-Padilla, Courtney A. Kase, Rachana Seelam, and Bradley D. Stein. 2018. "Unmet Mental Health Treatment Need and Attitudes toward Online Mental Health Services among Community College Students." *Psychiatric Services* 69 (5): 597–600. https://doi.org/10.1176/appi.ps.201700402.

Eichenberg, Christiane, and Markus Schott. 2017. "Serious Games for Psychotherapy: A Systematic Review." *Games for Health Journal* 6 (3): 127–135. https://doi.org/10.1089/g4h.2016.0068.

Ferris, Amber L., and Erin E. Hollenbaugh. 2018. "A Uses and Gratifications Approach to Exploring Antecedents to Facebook Dependency." *Journal of Broadcasting & Electronic Media* 62 (1): 51–70. https://doi.org/10.1080/08838151.2017.1375501.

Gerbner, George. 1970. "Cultural Indicators: The Case of Violence in Television Drama." *The Annals of the American Academy of Political and Social Science* 388 (1): 69–81. https://doi.org/10.1177/000271627038800108.

Gerbner, George, Larry Gross, Michael Morgan, and Nancy Signorielli. 1986. "Living with Television: The Dynamics of the Cultivation Process." In *Perspectives on Media Effects*, edited by Jennings Bryant and Dolf Zillman, 17–40. Hilldale: Lawrence Erlbaum Associates.

Gerbner, George, Larry Gross, Michael Morgan, Nancy Signorielli, and James Shanahan. 2002. "Growing Up with Television: Cultivation Process." In *Media Effects: Advances in Theory and Research*, 2nd ed., edited by Jennings Bryant and Dolf Zillmann, 43–67. New York: Lawrence Elbaum Associates, Inc.

Giddens, Anthony. 1992. *The Transformation of Intimacy: Sexuality, Love and Eroticism in Modern Societies* (Nachdr.). Stanford: Stanford University Press.

Golbeck, Jennifer. 2017. "Are You a Social Media Addict?" *Psychology Today*, September 26, 2017. https://www.psychologytoday.com/us/blog/your-online-secrets/201709/are-you-social-media-addict.

Gould, Madelyn S., Jimmie Lou Harris Munfakh, Keri Lubell, Marjorie Kleinman, and Sarah Parker. 2002. "Seeking Help from the Internet during Adolescence." *Journal of the American Academy of Child & Adolescent Psychiatry* 41 (10): 1182–1189. https://doi.org/10.1097/00004583-200210000-00007.

Granovetter, Mark S. 1973. "The Strength of Weak Ties." *American Journal of Sociology* 78 (6): 1360–1380. https://edisciplinas.usp.br/pluginfile.php/4865899/mod_resource/content/0/The%20Strength%20of%20Weak%20Ties.pdf.

Greenberg, Bradley S. 1974. "Gratifications of Television Viewing and Their Correlates for British Children." In *The Uses of Mass Communications: Current Perspectives on Gratifications Research*, edited by Jay G. Blumler and Elihu Katz, 71–92. Beverly Hills: Sage.

Greene, Jeremy A., Niteesh K. Choudhry, Elaine Kilabuk, and William H. Shrank. 2011. "Online Social Networking by Patients with Diabetes: A Qualitative Evaluation of Communication with Facebook." *Journal of General Internal Medicine* 26 (3): 287–292. https://doi.org/10.1007/s11606-010-1526-3.

Greidanus, Elaine, and Robin D. Everall. 2010. "Helper Therapy in an Online Suicide Prevention Community." *British Journal of Guidance & Counselling* 38 (2): 191–204. https://doi.org/10.1080/03069881003600991.

Guaiana, Giuseppe, Julia Mastrangelo, Shawn Hendrikx, and Corrado Barbui. 2021. "A Systematic Review of the Use of Telepsychiatry in Depression." *Community Mental Health Journal* 57 (1): 93–100. https://doi.org/10.1007/s10597-020-00724-2.

Gustafson, David H., Robert Hawkins, Suzanne Pingree, Fiona McTavish, Neeraj K. Arora, John Mendenhall, David F. Cella et al. 2001. "Effect of Computer Support on Younger Women with Breast Cancer." *Journal of General Internal Medicine* 16 (7): 435–445. https://doi: 10.1046/j.1525-1497.2001.016007435.x.

Gutman, Rachel. 2018. "Reddit's Case for Anonymity on the Internet." *The Atlantic*, June 28, 2018. https://www.theatlantic.com/technology/archive/2018/06/reddit-anonymity-privacy-authenticity/564071/.

Guynn, Jessica. 2016. "Facebook Groups Reaches 1 Billion Users." *USA Today*, January 27, 2016. https://www.usatoday.com/story/tech/news/2016/01/27/facebook-groups-reaches-1-billion-users/79414710/.

Harper, Everett. 2016. "Weak Ties Matter." *TechCrunch*, April 26, 2016. https://social.techcrunch.com/2016/04/26/weak-ties-matter/.

Hempstead, Karen Elaine. 2015. "Motivation Themes: Achievement, Affiliation, and Power in 'Sesame Street' From 1969–2013." Fielding Graduate University ProQuest Dissertations 3707172. https://www.proquest.com/openview/71a1cba5231dbf539d8948ce89719d3a/1?pq-origsite=gscholar&cbl=18750.

Henderson, Will, and Mary Jackson Pitts. 2019. "A Therapeutic Role of Online Communities." A paper presented at the Southern States Communication Association Conference at Montgomery, Alabama, April, 2019.

Hesse, Bradford W., David E. Nelson, Gary L. Kreps, Robert T. Croyle, Neeraj K. Arora, Barbara K. Rimer, and Kasisomayajula Viswanath. 2005. "Trust and Sources of Health Information: The Impact of the Internet and Its Implications for Health Care Providers: Findings from the First Health Information National Trends

Survey." *Archives of Internal Medicine* 165 (22): 2618–2624. https://doi.org/10.1001/archinte.165.22.2618.

Hillery, George A. 1955. "Definition of Community." *Rural Sociology* 20 (2): 111–123.

History.com Editors. 2010. "The Mayflower." A&E Television Networks, LLC., and the Arena Group, original date March 4, 2010; updated November 15, 2021. https://www.history.com/topics/colonial-america/mayflower.

Holden, Constance. 1972. "TV Violence: Government Study Yields More Evidence, No Verdict." *Science* 175 (4022): 608–611. http://www.jstor.org/stable/1732921.

Horst, Heather A., and Daniel Miller. 2012. *Digital Anthropology*. London: Bloomsbury Academic.

Hutchinson, Andrew. 2020. "Reddit Reports that it Now Sees 52 Million Daily Active Users." *Social Media Today*, December 1, 2020. https://www.socialmediatoday.com/news/reddit-reports-that-it-now-sees-52-million-daily-active-users/589922/.

Igartua, Juan-José, Félix Ortega-Mohedano, and Carlos Arcila-Calderón. 2020. "Communication Use in the Times of the Coronavirus: A Cross-Cultural Study// Usos de la Comunicación en los Tiempos del Coronavirus. Un Estudio Transcultural." *Profesional de la Información* 29 (3). http://eprints.rclis.org/40135/1/igartua-ortega-arcila.pdf.

Iqbal, Mansoor. 2021. "Facebook Revenue and Usage Statistics (2021)." *Business of Apps*, January 19, 2022. https://www.businessofapps.com/data/facebook-statistics/.

Isaranon, Yokfah. 2019. "The Role of Facebook Affirmation towards Ideal Self-Image and Self-Esteem." *The Journal of Behavioral Science* (14): 46–62. https://so06.tci-thaijo.org/index.php/IJBS/article/view/140397/121439.

Ivey-Stephenson, Asha Z., Zewditu Demissie, Alexander E. Crosby, Deborah M. Stone, Elizabeth Gaylor, Natalie Wilkins, Richard Lowry, and Margaret Brown. 2020. "Suicidal Ideation and Behaviors among High School Students—Youth Risk Behavior Survey, United States, 2019." *MMWR Supplements* 69 (1): 47. http://doi.org/10.15585/mmwr.su6901a6.

Jamieson, Lynn. 1999. "Intimacy Transformed? A Critical Look at the 'Pure Relationship'." *Sociology* 33 (3): 477–494. https://doi.org/10.1177/S0038038599000310.

Jenson, Joli. 1990. *Redeeming Modernity: Contradictions in Media Criticism*. London: Sage Publishing.

Katz, Elihu, Jay G. Blumler, and Michael Gurevitch. 1973. "Uses and Gratifications Research." *Public Opinion Quarterly* 37 (4, Winter): 509–523. https://doi.org/10.1086/268109.

Katz, Elihu, Michael Gurevitch, and Hadassah Haas.1973. "On the Use of the Mass Media for Important Things." *American Sociological Review* 38 (2): 164–181. https://doi.org/10.2307/2094393.

Kemp, Simon. 2018. "Reddit Now Has More Active Users than Twitter—And is More Engaging than Porn." *TNW*, April 19, 2018. https://thenextweb.com/news/reddit-now-active-users-twitter-engaging-porn.

Kemp, Simon. 2020. "Digital 2020: 3.8 Billion People Use Social Media." *We Are Social Ltd.*, January 30, 2020. https://wearesocial.com/uk/blog/2020/01/digital-2020-3-8-billion-people-use-social-media/.

Kessler, Ronald C., Kristin D. Mickelson, and Shanyang Zhao. 1997. "Patterns and Correlates of Self-Help Group Membership." *American Psychologist* 27 (3): 27–46. http://midus.wisc.edu/findings/pdfs/53.pdf.

Kim, Joongsub, and Rachel Kaplan. 2004. "Physical and Psychological Factors in Sense of Community: New Urbanist Kentlands and Nearby Orchard Village." *Environment and Behavior* 36 (3): 313–340. https://journals-sagepub-com.libproxy.clemson.edu/doi/10.1177/0013916503260236.

Kingod, Natasja, Bryan Cleal, Ayo Wahlberg, and Gitte R. Husted. 2017. "Online Peer-to-Peer Communities in the Daily Lives of People with Chronic Illness: A Qualitative Systematic Review." *Qualitative Health Research* 27 (1): 89–99. https://doi.org/10.1177/1049732316680203.

Kross, Ethan, Philippe Verduyn, Emre Demiralp, Jiyoung Park, David Seungjae Lee, Natalie Lin, Holly Shablack, John Jonides, and Oscar Ybarra. 2013. "Facebook Use Predicts Declines in Subjective Well-Being in Young Adults." *PloS One* 8 (8): e69841. https://doi.org/10.1371/journal.pone.0069841.

Kumashiro, Madoka, Caryl E. Rusbult, Catrin Finkenauer, and Shevaun L. Stocker. 2007. "To Think or To Do: The Impact of Assessment and Locomotion Orientation on the Michelangelo Phenomenon." *Journal of Social and Personal Relationships* 24 (4): 591–611. https://doi.org/10.1177/0265407507079261.

Lal, Shalini, and Carol E. Adair. 2014. "E-Mental Health: A Rapid Review of the Literature." *Psychiatric Services* 65 (1): 24–32. https://doi.org/10.1176/appi.ps.201300009.

Leary, Mark R. 1990. "Responses to Social Exclusion: Social Anxiety, Jealousy, Loneliness, Depression, and Low Self-Esteem." *Journal of Social and Clinical Psychology* 9 (2): 221–229. https://doi.org/10.1521/jscp.1990.9.2.221.

Lee, Riley. 2017. "How a Facebook Group Helped Me in My Battle with Depression." *The Mighty*, January 3, 2017. https://themighty.com/2017/01/facebook-groups-helps-me-with-depression/.

Lerman, Bethany I., Stephen P. Lewis, Margaret Lumley, Greg J. Grogan, Chloe C. Hudson, and Erin Johnson. 2017. "Teen Depression Groups on Facebook: A Content Analysis." *Journal of Adolescent Research* 32 (6): 719–741. https://doi.org/10.1177/0743558416673717.

Levy, Mark R., and Sven Windahl. 1985. "Audience Activity and Gratifications: A Conceptual Clarification and Exploration." In *Media Gratifications Research: Current Perspectives*, edited by Karl Erik Rosengren, Lawrence A. Wenner, and Philip Palmgreen, 111. Beverly Hills: Sage Publications.

Lexico. 2022. s.v. "Subreddit." https://www.lexico.com/en/definition/subreddit.

Lian, Olaug S., and Sarah Nettleton. 2015. "'United We Stand': Framing Myalgic Encephalomyelitis in a Virtual Symbolic Community." *Qualitative Health Research* 25 (10): 1383–1394. https://doi.org/10.1177/1049732314562893.

Lieberman, Morton A., Mitch Golant, Janine Giese-Davis, Andy Winzlenberg, Harold Benjamin, Keith Humphreys, Carol Kronenwetter, Stefani Russo, and David Spiegel. 2003. "Electronic Support Groups for Breast Carcinoma: A Clinical Trial of Effectiveness." *Cancer: Interdisciplinary International Journal of the American Cancer Society* 97 (4): 920–925. https://doi.org/10.1002/cncr.11145.

Lijadi, Anastasia Aldelina, and Gertina Johanna van Schalkwyk. 2015. "Online Facebook Focus Group Research of Hard-to-Reach Participants." *International Journal of Qualitative Methods* 14 (5). https://doi.org/10.1177/1609406915621383.

Lin, Carolyn A. 1996. "Standpoint: Looking Back: The Contribution of Blumler and Katz's Uses of Mass Communication to Communication Research." *Journal of Broadcasting & Electronic Media* 40 (4): 574–581. https://doi-org.ezproxy.library.astate.edu/10.1080/08838159609364379.

Liu, C.-T., and Guo, Y. M. 2015. "The Role of Sense of Belonging in Social Media Usage: A Tale of Two Types of Users." *Asia Pacific Journal of Information Systems* 25 (2): 403–422. https://doi.org/10.14329/apjis.2015.25.2.403.

Liu, Dong, and Roy F. Baumeister. 2016. "Social Networking Online and Personality of Self-Worth: A Meta-Analysis." *Journal of Research in Personality* 64: 79–89. https://doi.org/10.1016/j.jrp.2016.06.024.

Lobchuk, Michelle, Susan McClement, Maureen Rigney, Amy Copeland, and Hamideh Bayrampour. 2015. "A Qualitative Analysis of 'Naturalistic' Conversations in a Peer-Led Online Support Community for Lung Cancer." *Cancer Nursing* 38 (5): E21–E31. https://doi.org/10.1097/NCC.0000000000000207.

Lomsky-Feder, Edna. 2004. "Life Stories, War, and Veterans: On the Social Distribution of Memories." *Ethos* 32 (1): 82–109. https://psycnet.apa.org/doi/10.1525/eth.2004.32.1.82.

Mares, Marie-Louise, and Zhongdang Pan. 2013. "Effects of Sesame Street: A Meta-Analysis of Children's Learning in 15 Countries." *Journal of Applied Developmental Psychology* 34 (3): 140–151. https://doi.org/10.1016/j.appdev.2013.01.001.

McLeod, Jack M., and Lee B. Becker. 1974. "Testing the Validity of Gratification Measures through Political Effects Analysis." In *The Uses of Mass Communications*, edited by Jay G. Blumler and Elihu Katz, 137–166. Beverly Hills: Sage.

McLuhan, Marshall. 1964. *Understanding Media: The Extension of Man.* New York: McGraw Hill Book Company.

McQuail, Denis, and Michael Gurevitch. 1974. "Explaining Audience Behavior: Three Approaches Considered." In *The Uses of Mass Communications: Current Perspectives on Gratifications Research* 3, edited by Jay G. Blumler and Elihu Katz, 287–301. Beverly Hills: Sage.

Medlock, Stephanie, Saeid Eslami, Marjan Askari, Derk L. Arts, Danielle Sent, Sophia E. De Rooij, and Ameen Abu-Hanna. 2015. "Health Information–Seeking Behavior of Seniors Who Use the Internet: A Survey." *Journal of Medical Internet Research* 17 (1): e3749. https://doi.org/10.2196/jmir.3749.

META. 2021a. Screenshot sourced from https://www.facebook.com/search/top?q=depression. 2021.

META. 2021b. Screenshot sourced from https://www.facebook.com/emotional_health. 2021.

META. 2022. "What Are the Privacy Options for Facebook Groups?" *Facebook Help Center*. https://www.facebook.com/help/220336891328465.

Mickelson, Kristen D. 1997. "Seeking Social Support: Parents in Electronic Support Groups." In *Culture of the Internet*, edited by S. Kiesler (Ed.), 157–178. Mahwah: Lawrence Erlbaum Associates Publishers.

Morin, Amy. 2019. "Depression Statistics Everyone Should Know." *Verywell Mind*, Updated May 11, 2021. https://www.verywellmind.com/depression-statistics-everyone-should-know-4159056.

Nelson, Eve-Lynn, Martha Barnard, and Sharon Cain. 2003. "Treating Childhood Depression over Videoconferencing." *Telemedicine Journal and E-Health* 9 (1): 49–55. https://doi.org/10.1089/153056203763317648.

Nesi, Jacqueline. 2020. "The Impact of Social Media on Youth Mental Health: Challenges and Opportunities." *North Carolina Medical Journal* 81 (2): 116–121. http://www.ncmedicaljournal.com/content/81/2/116.

New International Version. 2011. *The Holy Bible*. Biblica Inc. https://www.biblegateway.com/versions/New-International-Version-NIV-Bible/.

Ngak, Chenda. 2001. "Then and Now: A History of Social Networking Sites." *CBS News*, July 6, 2001. https://www.cbsnews.com/pictures/then-and-now-a-history-of-social-networking-sites/.

Nielsen, Annegrete Juul, and Lone Grøn.2012. "Standardising the Lay: Logics of Change in Programs of Disease Self-Management." *Culture Unbound* 4 (3): 425–442. https://doi.org/10.3384/cu.2000.1525.124425.

NIMH. 2021. "Mental Illness." *National Institute of Mental Illness*, January 2021. https://www.nimh.nih.gov/health/statistics/mental-illness.shtml.

Norman, Cameron, Scott McIntosh, Peter Selby, and Gunther Eysenbach. 2008. "Web-Assisted Tobacco Interventions: Empowering Change in the Global Fight for the Public's (e) Health." *Journal of Medical Internet Research* 10 (5): e48. https://doi.org/10.2196/jmir.1171.

Novet, Jordan. 2019. "Microsoft Paid $26 Billion for LinkedIn, Then Mostly Left it Alone—And CEO Jeff Weiner is Good with That." *CNBC*, December 27, 2019. https://www.cnbc.com/2019/12/27/linkedin-ceo-jeff-weiner-is-ok-with-microsofts-hands-off-approach.html.

Oliver, Debra Parker, Karla Washington, Elaine Wittenberg-Lyles, Ashley Gage, Megan Mooney, and George Demiris. 2015. "Lessons Learned from a Secret Facebook Support Group." *Health & Social Work* 40 (2): 125–133. https://doi.org/10.1093/hsw/hlv007.

Papacharissi, Zizi. 2009. "Uses and Gratifications." In *An Integrated Approach to Communication Theory and Research*, edited by Don W. Stacks and Michael Brian Salwen, 137–152. London; New York: Routledge.

Peng, Wei, Aurora Occa, Soroya Julian McFarlane, and Susan E. Morgan. 2019. "A Content Analysis of the Discussions about Clinical Trials on a Cancer-Dedicated Online Forum." *Journal of Health Communication* 24 (12): 912–922. https://doi.org/10.1080/10810730.2019.1688895.

Phillips, Sarah. 2007. "A Brief History of Facebook." *The Guardian*, July 25, 2007. http://www.theguardian.com/technology/2007/jul/25/media.newmedia.

Preece, Jennifer 1998. "Empathic Communities: Offering Support and Sharing Information in a Bulletin Board Community." Paper presented at the UK CVE Conference, June 17–9.

Preece, Jennifer J., and Kambiz Ghozati. 2001. "Experiencing Empathy On-Line." In *The Internet and Health Communication: Experiences and Expectations*, edited by R. E. Rice and J. E. Katz, 237–260. Thousand Oaks: Sage.

Reddit. 2006. "r/science." Reddit Inc., created October 16, 2006. https://www.reddit.com/r/science/.

Reddit. 2008. "r/philosophy." Reddit Inc., created January 25, 2008. https://www.reddit.com/r/philosophy/

Reddit. 2008a. "r/pics." Reddit Inc., created January 25, 2008. https://www.reddit.com/r/pics/.

Reddit. 2008b. "r/psychology." Reddit Inc., created March 8, 2008. https://www.reddit.com/r/psychology/

Reddit. 2008c. "r/Documentaries." Reddit Inc., created March 21, 2008. https://www.reddit.com/r/Documentaries/.

Reddit. 2008d. "r/selfhelp." Reddit Inc., created March 27, 2008. https://www.reddit.com/r/selfhelp/.

Reddit. 2008e. "r/mentalhealth." Reddit Inc., created June 12, 2008. https://www.reddit.com/r/mentalhealth/.

Reddit. 2008f. "r/Anxiety." Reddit Inc., created September 15, 2008. https://www.reddit.com/r/Anxiety/.

Reddit. 2008g. "r/ADHD." Reddit Inc., created October 28, 2008. https://www.reddit.com/r/ADHD/.

Reddit. 2008h. "r/SuicideWatch." Reddit Inc., created December 16, 2008. https://www.reddit.com/r/SuicideWatch/.

Reddit. 2008i. "r/SuicideWatch: What to Expect When Calling a Hotline." Reddit Inc., https://www.reddit.com/r/SuicideWatch/wiki/hotlines.

Reddit. 2009. "r/depression." Reddit Inc., created January 1, 2009. https://www.reddit.com/r/depression/.

Reddit. 2009a. "r/Accounting." Reddit Inc., created April 4, 2009. https://www.reddit.com/r/Accounting/.

Reddit. 2009b. "r/BipolarReddit." Reddit Inc., created June 4, 2009. https://www.reddit.com/r/BipolarReddit/.

Reddit. 2010. "r/GetMotivated." Reddit Inc., created March 27, 2010. https://www.reddit.com/r/GetMotivated/.

Reddit. 2010a. "SWResources: Worried about someone who may be suicidal? Here's some info about how to assess risk." Reddit Inc., created May 11, 2010. https://www.reddit.com/r/SWResources/comments/igh87/concerned_but_dont_know_what_to_say_here_are_some/.

Reddit. 2010b. "r/getting_over_it." Reddit Inc., created June 7, 2010. https://www.reddit.com/r/getting_over_it/.

Reddit. 2010c. "r/foreveralone." Reddit Inc., created September 15, 2010. https://www.reddit.com/r/ForeverAlone/.

Reddit. 2011. "r/StopSelfHarm." Reddit Inc., created May 23, 2011. https://www.reddit.com/r/StopSelfHarm/.

Reddit. 2012. "r/SampleSize." Reddit Inc., created February 21, 2012. https://www.reddit.com/r/SampleSize/.

Reddit. 2012a. "r/MadeMeSmile." Reddit Inc., created August 10, 2012. https://www.reddit.com/r/MadeMeSmile/.

Reddit. 2014. "Depression Help." Reddit Inc., created January 26, 2014. https://www.reddit.com/r/depression_help/.

Reddit. 2014a. "F— Eating Disorders." Reddit Inc., created November 14, 2014. https://www.reddit.com/r/fuckeatingdisorders/.

Reddit. 2021. Screenshot sourced from https://www.reddit.com/. 2021.

Reinert, Maddy, Theresa Nguyen, and Danielle Fritze. 2017. "The State of Mental Health in America." *Mental Health America*, December 18, 2017. https://mhanational.org/sites/default/files/2021%20State%20of%20Mental%20Health%20in%20America_0.pdf.

Robinson, David. 1988. "Self-Help Groups." In *Small Group Communication: A Reader*, 5th ed., edited by Robert S. Cathcart and Larry A. Samovar, 117–129. Dubuque: Wm. C. Brown.

Rodham, Karen, Jeff Gavin, and Meriel Miles. 2007. "I Hear, I Listen and I Care: A Qualitative Investigation into the Function of a Self-Harm Message Board." *Suicide and Life-Threatening Behavior* 37 (4): 422–430. https://www.proquest.com/openview/f215899071569fdf95b8a59acd2538e8/1?pq-origsite=gscholar&cbl=6058.

Rodriguez, Salvador. 2020. "Mark Zuckerberg Shifted Facebook's Focus to Groups after the 2016 Election, and It's Changed How People Use the Site." *CNBC*, February 16, 2020. https://www.cnbc.com/2020/02/16/zuckerbergs-focus-on-facebook-groups-increases-facebook-engagement.html.

Rovai, Alfred. 2002. "Building Sense of Community at a Distance." *International Review of Research in Open and Distance Learning*. https://doi.org/10.19173/irrodl.v3i1.79.

Ruggiero, Thomas. E. 2000. "Uses and Gratifications Theory in the 21st Century." *Mass Communication & Society* 3 (1): 3–37. https://doi-org.ezproxy.library.astate.edu/10.1207/S15327825MCS0301_02.

SAMHSA. 2019. *Results from the 2019 National Survey on Drug Use and Health: Graphics from the Key Findings Report*. Center for Behavioral Health Statistics and Quality Substance Abuse and Mental Health Services Administration U.S. Department of Health and Human Services. https://www.samhsa.gov/data/sites/default/files/reports/rpt29393/2019NSDUHFFRBriefSlides082120.pdf.

Sandler, Piper. 2020. "Taking Stock With Teens®—Fall 2020." Piper Sandler Companies. https://www.pipersandler.com/3col.aspx?id=6039.

Schachter, Robert. 2011. "Using the Group in Cognitive Group Therapy." *Group* 35 (2): 135–149. https://www.jstor.org/stable/41716126.

Schramm, William, Edwin B. Parker and Jack Lylē. 1961. *Television in the Lives of Children*. Stanford: Stanford University Press.

Shahab, Lion, and Andy McEwen. 2009. "Online Support for Smoking Cessation: A Systematic Review of the Literature." *Addiction* (Abingdon, England) 104 (11): 1792–1804. https://doi.org/10.1111/j.1360-0443.2009.02710.x.

Shakya, Holly B., and Nicholas A. Christakis. 2017. "A New, More Rigorous Study Confirms: The More You Use Facebook, the Worse You Feel." *Harvard Business Review*, April 10, 2017. https://hbr.org/2017/04/a-new-more-rigorous-study-confirms-the-more-you-use-facebook-the-worse-you-feel.

Slone, Norah C., Robert J. Reese, and Michael J. McClellan. 2012. "Telepsychology Outcome Research with Children and Adolescents: A Review of the Literature." *Psychological Services* 9 (3): 272. http://doi.org/10.1037/a0027607.

Smith, Aaron, and Monica Anderson. 2018. "Social Media Use in 2018." *Pew Research, Inc.*, March 1, 2018. https://www.pewresearch.org/internet/2018/03/01/social-media-use-in-2018/.

Smith, Freya, Christian Jones, Fergus Gracey, Ricky Mullis, Neil Stewart Coulson, and Anna De Simoni. 2021. "Emotional Adjustment Post-Stroke: A Qualitative Study of an Online Stroke Community." *Neuropsychological Rehabilitation* 31 (3): 414–431. https://doi.org/10.1080/09602011.2019.1702561.

Strand, Monica, Lillian Sofie Eng, and Deede Gammon. 2020. "Combining Online and Off-line Peer Support Groups in Community Mental Health Care Settings: A Qualitative Study of Service Users' Experiences." *International Journal of Mental Health Systems* 14 (1): 1–12. https://ijmhs.biomedcentral.com/articles/10.1186/s13033-020-00370-x.

Strauss, Anselm L., and Barney G. Glaser. 1975. *Chronic Illness and the Quality of Life*. St. Louis: Mosby.

Swan, Melanie. 2012. "Crowdsourced Health Research Studies: An Important Emerging Complement to Clinical Trials in the Public Health Research Ecosystem." *Journal of Medical Internet Research* 14 (2): e1988. https://doi.org/10.2196/jmir.1988.

Tartaglia, Stefano. 2016. "Different Modalities of Using Facebook: The Influence of Actual Social Relations, Wellbeing, and Attitude towards the Medium." *Studia Psychologica* 58 (1): 3–17. https://doi.org/10.21909/sp.2016.01.703.

The Gilder Lehrman Institute of American History. 2013. *Coming to America on the Mayflower*. https://www.gilderlehrman.org/sites/default/files/inline-pdfs/Coming%20to%20America%20on%20the%20Mayflower.pdf.

Tönnies, Ferdinand. 1957. *Community and Society*. East Lansing: Michigan State University Press.

Twenge, Jean M., A. Bell Cooper, Thomas E. Joiner, Mary E. Duffy, and Sarah G. Binau. 2019. "Age, Period, and Cohort Trends in Mood Disorder Indicators and Suicide-Related Outcomes in a Nationally Representative Dataset, 2005–2017." *Journal of Abnormal Psychology* 128 (3): 185. https://doi.apa.org/doi/10.1037/abn0000410.

United States National Institute of Mental Health (U.S.). 1972. *Television and Growing Up—The Impact of Television Violence—Report to the Surgeon General, United States Public Health Service, From the Surgeon General's Scientific Advisory Committee on Television and Social Behavior*. Rockville, MD: U.S. Dept. of Health, Education, and Welfare, Health Services and Mental Health Administration, National Institute of Mental Health. https://www.ojp.gov/ncjrs/virtual-library/abstracts/television-and-growing-impact-televised-violence-report-surgeon.

US Centers for Disease Control and Prevention. 2012. "Youth Risk Behavior Surveillance System (YRBSS)." https://www.cdc.gov/healthyyouth/data/yrbs/index.htm.

Valenzuela, Sebastián, Namsu Park, and Kerk F. Kee. 2009. "Is There Social Capital in a Social Network Site?: Facebook Use and College Students' Life Satisfaction,

Trust, and Participation." *Journal of Computer-Mediated Communication* 14 (4): 875–901. https://doi.org/10.1111/j.1083-6101.2009.01474.x.
Valkenburg, Patti M., and Jessica Tayor Piotrowski. 2017. *Plugged In: How Media Attract and Affect Youth.* New Haven; London: Yale University Press. https://yalebooks.yale.edu/sites/default/files/files/Media/9780300228090_UPDF.pdf.
Wallace, Patricia. 1999. *The Psychology of the Internet.* College Park: University of Maryland. https://doi.org/10.1017/CBO9780511581670.
Walther, Joseph B., and Sharon Boyd. 2002. "Attraction to Computer-Mediated Social Support." In *Communication Technology and Society: Audience Adoption and Uses*, edited by Carolyn A. Lin and David J. Atkin, 153–188. New York: Hampton Press.
Walsh, Casey A., and Morhaf Al Achkar. 2021. "A Qualitative Study of Online Support Communities for Lung Cancer Survivors on Targeted Therapies." *Supportive Care in Cancer* 29: 4493–4500. https://doi.org/10.1007/s00520-021-05989-1.
Weinberg, Nancy, John D. Schmale, Janet Uken, and Keith Wessel. 1995. "Computer-Mediated Support Groups." *Social Work with Groups* 17 (4): 43–54. https://doi.org/10.1300/J009V17N04_04.
Wenner, Lawrence A., Philip Palmgreen, and Karl Erik Rosengren. 1985. "Uses and Gratifications Research: The Past Ten Years." In *Media Gratifications Research: Current Perspectives*, edited by Lawrence A. Wenner, Philip Palmgreen, and Karl Erik Rosengren, 11–37. Beverly Hills: Sage Publications.
Williams, Aya, Rachel LaRocca, Trina Chang, Nhi-Ha Trinh, Maurizio Fava, Joseph Kvedar, and Albert Yeung. 2014. "Web-Based Depression Screening and Psychiatric Consultation for College Students: A Feasibility and Acceptability Study." *International Journal of Telemedicine and Applications* Vol. 2014: #580786. https://doi.org/10.1155/2014/580786.
Willis, Olivia. 2018. "When Illness Means Facebook Becomes a 'Safe Space'." *ABC News*, February 26, 2018. https://www.abc.net.au/news/health/2018-02-27/how-social-media-is-connecting-people-living-with-illness/9484574.
Wimmer, Roger D., and Joseph R. Dominick. 2013. *Mass Media Research: An Introduction*, 10th ed. Belmont: Wadsworth.
Winzelberg, Andrew J., Catherine Classen, Georg W. Alpers, Heidi Roberts, Cheryl Koopman, Robert E. Adams, Heidemarie Ernst, Parvati Dev, and C. Barr Taylor. 2003. "Evaluation of an Internet Support Group for Women with Primary Breast Cancer." *Cancer: Interdisciplinary International Journal of the American Cancer Society* 97 (5): 1164–1173. https://doi.org/10.1002/cncr.11174.
Wright, Kevin. 2000. "Perceptions of On-Line Support Providers: An Examination of Perceived Homophily, Source Credibility, Communication and Social Support Within On-Line Support Groups." *Communication Quarterly* 48 (1): 44–59.
Wright, Kevin B., Sally B. Bell, Kevin B. Wright, and Sally B. Bell. 2003. "Health-Related Support Groups on the Internet: Linking Empirical Findings to Social Support and Computer-Mediated Communication Theory." *Journal of Health Psychology* 8 (1): 39–54. https://doi.org/10.1177%2F1359105303008001429.
Yalom, Irvin D., and Molyn Leszcz. 2008. *The Theory and Practice of Group Psychotherapy*, 5th ed. New York: Basic Books.

Ybarra, Michelle L., and William W. Eaton. 2005. Internet-Based Mental Health Interventions. *Mental Health Services Research* 7 (2): 75–87. https://doi.org/10.1007/s11020-005-3779-8.

Zhang, Shaodian, Erin O'Carroll Bantum, Jason Owen, Suzanne Bakken, and Noémie Elhadad. 2017. "Online Cancer Communities as Informatics Intervention for Social Support: Conceptualization, Characterization, and Impact." *Journal of the American Medical Informatics Association* 24 (2): 451–459. https://doi.org/10.1093/jamia/ocw093.

Index

About the Authors

Will Henderson has been involved with online communities since the early 2000s. His research surrounds online communities, social media activity, and experience tourism. Throughout his career, he has been involved in crafting numerous social media strategies for a variety of brands and nonprofits. Intertwining brand marketing and analytical research, Henderson provides a new perspective to the topic of online communities and online behavior. His academic positions have included associate director for the Social Media Listening Center and lecturer at Clemson University. Henderson has also been involved in the Parks, Recreation and Tourism Management PhD Program at Clemson University. In addition to his research and contributions to academia, he is a mental health advocate. His hope is that this research will assist with developing new methods of recovery.

Dr. Mary Jackson Pitts focuses her research on media platforms and how these platforms can be used by organizations and people to address social, economic, educational, and political issues in society. Pitts serves as a professor at Arkansas State University (ASU) where she is the creative media production program coordinator and a senior professor in the Masters in Media Management program where her teaching focuses on communication theory, audience market analysis, entrepreneurship, and management. Over the course of more than thirty years of academic tenure, her research has addressed social media communities in higher education, personal branding, social media advertising endorsements, media management adaptability, and the use of new technologies to improve audience engagement among legacy and nonlegacy media, along with research in the area of political communication within social media platforms. Dr. Jackson Pitts is involved in the assessment of program outcomes and has been instrumental in the redesign and redevelopment of assessment tools and curriculum renovation. Dr. Jackson Pitts has been a faculty member at ASU since 1988.

www.ingramcontent.com/pod-product-compliance
Ingram Content Group UK Ltd.
Pitfield, Milton Keynes, MK11 3LW, UK
UKHW041839031026
15587UKWH00002B/877

9 781793 631022